LaFosse & Alexander's

ESSENTIAL BOOK OF
ORIGAMI

Become a Better Folder Through
16 Clear Lessons, Beginner to Intermediate

THE COMPLETE GUIDE
FOR EVERYONE

By Michael G. LaFosse and Richard L. Alexander, Origamido, Inc.

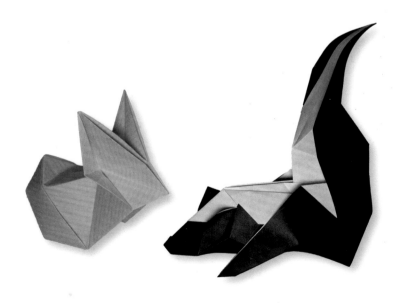

TUTTLE Publishing

Tokyo | Rutland, Vermont | Singapore

contents

The Projects

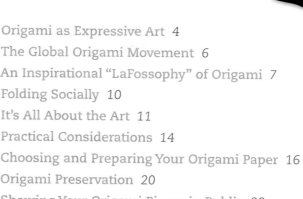

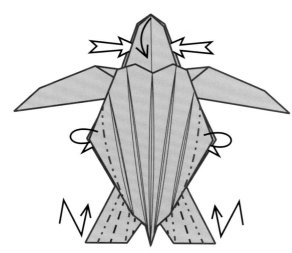
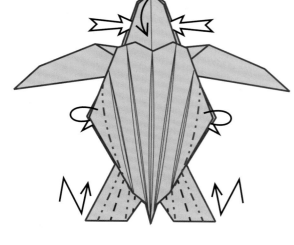

Dedication

We lovingly dedicate this collection of origami lessons to our dear friends and mentors, Mrs. Kyoko Kondo and Dr. Shigeo Kondo. Kyoko has been a lifelong, enthusiastic, international ambassador of origami, having served the national organization OrigamiUSA in many capacities for decades. She and Shigeo have personally nurtured countless folders and artists by attending their events and purchasing their art and publications. This unwavering support was essential to our becoming professional origami designers, authors and teachers. As a former Suzuki Method violin teacher, Kyoko knows well the importance and effectiveness of guided practice in any art. We hope you enjoy sharing these origami lessons with your students, just as Kyoko and Shigeo have shared so much with so many for so long!

Origami as Expressive Art

FOREWORD BY ORIGAMIDO STUDIO COFOUNDER RICHARD L. ALEXANDER

Origami as an expressive art form is relatively new, and in the last few decades has been marked by astounding innovation. This excitement is why Michael LaFosse and I founded Origamido Studio in 1996. There, we have been able to share our joy of designing and folding origami art through publishing, teaching and hosting hand-paper making workshops with other folding colleagues and artists. Michael named our studio "Origamido," which is Japanese for "fold – paper – school." The "do" suffix implies a long-term, dedicated study. Michael was familiar with this because his father learned Judo in the US Air Force (and later became an instructor himself), and Michael has also studied Taekwondo for over forty years. Many of our paper-folding students and customers share the "do" — that lifelong passion for origami. To us, it is much more than a hobby, and we have dozens of friends who use their annual vacation time to attend folding conventions now held all around the world.

What is origami art, and why might you want to study it? Although the invention of paper was documented in China about two thousand years ago, paper folding as a pastime seems to be only a few hundred years old. Until the last century, only a handful of objects were realized. It was (and still is) often dismissed as a trivial amusement for children. At best it was considered a folk craft.

Only since about the middle

of the twentieth century has origami exploded in popularity, and there is now a class of paper folding that clearly rises above the craft level. We define origami art as folded paper that expresses the human spirit. So many artists now express emotions so elegantly through folded paper that major museums are booking origami masterworks presented as creative and expressive art, and attendance is raising eyebrows in the art world. Why is this so?

Michael once opened a public presentation with this thought: "Art reveals the unique and complex nature of expressive human beings. Origami is one of those art forms that appeals to both the logical and the emotional needs of the mind." This richness of exploring the potential of the folded square spans the gamut, from single-fold sculptures to multi-piece geometric constructions illustrating concepts of higher mathematics. The Internet now makes it possible for such a previously obscure art form to become recognized and appreciated by a huge audience. Paper folding can and does efficiently provide a fertile field for a lifetime of enjoyable exploration and study for millions of people.

It is worth noting that most of our regular students are often proficient in other disciplines of the arts and sciences as well. Their backgrounds may include writing, engineering, mathematics, painting, photography, dance or music... and the mastery of any such endeavor benefits from a system-

atic approach to study and practice. Mathematicians love to solve puzzles to keep their reasoning skills sharp. Musicians practice scales and arpeggios to achieve and maintain technical competence. So too should origami students practice certain models to perfect and maintain essential folding skills. The benefit of doing so is proficiency, the gatekeeper of artistry. The value of many arts is often in the process itself, and that is certainly true with paper folding, where expression is not only in the final, folded form, but also in the beauty of the performance or the magic of the transformation during the folding sequence.

Origami artists come to work with us at Origamido Studio to improve their artistry. Lessons don't only involve acquiring technical folding skills; sometimes they include help with choosing appropriate papers. In the world of origami art, the "look" of a piece of folded art is much more than just its physical appearance. Much of that look depends upon the intrinsic qualities of the chosen paper. Qualities such as strength or thinness may be critical to accommodating multiple layers, or subtle shaping to convey attitude or gestures.

Many artists simply love to learn more about the medium of paper and its fibers, in order to master the technical skills necessary to fold more artfully. We use a palette of strong plant fibers of many different types and qualities (soft and supple, to hard and rigid). Compromises can

be maddening for artists, and so the ability to come to Origamido Studio to customize the perfect batch of handmade paper for each specific work of folded art is a dream come true. Artists can choose, prepare, blend and pigment the highest quality of fibers to form sheets of the perfect size and thickness (or thinness).

If you are new to origami, we suggest that you start with our *Origami Studio* DVD kit for beginners (Tuttle Publishing). It features thirty projects to illustrate basic origami folds and techniques. If you have already enjoyed those, or other origami lessons for beginners, and you are interested in exploring the artistry of folding, then this selection of origami projects was designed for you! Each one is an *étude*, or brief study, designed or selected for the advancing student to complete in one sitting. It was important for us to select models that not only teach key folding skills, but are also fun for you to fold repeatedly until you have mastered those skills.

The Global Origami Movement

JOIN THE RANKS OF ARTFUL FOLDERS

BY ORIGAMIDO STUDIO COFOUNDERS MICHAEL G. LAFOSSE AND RICHARD L. ALEXANDER

Most people who fold paper for entertainment, decoration or fun consider origami a craft. There is also a growing segment focused on using origami to advance the understanding of science, math and engineering. A third cadre of origami enthusiasts is focused on "artful" folding, which has suddenly captivated a diverse and expanded audience. Never before have folded pieces of paper been appreciated as jaw-dropping art, exhibited not just at annual origami conventions (now held in several countries), but also at major art museums around the world. This global audience is now engaged in a healthy dialogue about folded art, providing the critical evaluation and response so important to the development and maturation of any art form.

Artful folding can, and does, provide a lifetime of enjoyment to many, but the advancing folder often experiences technical and artistic challenges. This can result in failure, and lead to disappointment or discouragement. Until the reasons for failure are identified, they cannot be corrected. Most origami books merely present diagrams to show how to fold a project, analogous to sheet music studied by a budding musician. While notation alone may get you through a song, it is invaluable to hear it performed properly, and even more helpful if you hear it performed artfully. Rapid progress can happen when you work with a qualified instructor. Similarly, many origami artists would benefit greatly by studying with a teacher — someone to guide his or her progress toward a better performance.

Since modern origami artistry is so new, there are relatively few resources or instructors who are qualified, willing and available to help other folding artists identify and overcome the most persistent and predictable problems. We have worked with hundreds of artists, and have used that experience to select each project to develop or improve a specific aspect of paper folding skill and artistry. By working through these lessons, you will be improving critical folding techniques, exploring origami design styles, and gaining insights into origami's instrument: the paper itself. In short, these are the things that must come together in the head and hands of today's expressive paper folding artist.

In addition, our demonstrations on the accompanying video DVD will help you understand the lessons well beyond what a collection of diagrams alone can do. We suggest that you watch a video lesson for the first time without folding, and then watch it again, this time with paper in hand, advancing the video lesson step-by-step at your own pace. Study and practice your origami artistry as if you were studying music. These lessons will help you diagnose the areas where you need more work. Assign yourself a new lesson each week. We hope that you will soon memorize, and then enjoy practicing the most applicable lessons. We wish you a most rewarding journey along your path to becoming a "better performer" — a more artful folder!

"Munich Orchids and Alexander Aztec Swallowtails" — Handmade Origamido papers by Alexander, original origami by LaFosse.

An Inspirational "LaFossophy" of Origami

OBSERVATIONS FROM THE STUDIO

BY ORIGAMIDO STUDIO COFOUNDER RICHARD L. ALEXANDER

One can't escape developing a philosophy around any subject studied passionately for a long time. I have begun to use, tongue-in-cheek, the term "LaFossophy," because I was at a loss for a word to adequately summarize Michael's wisdom that permeates the Origamido Studio. While the majority of our students know us from our publications, for decades we have also been teaching all levels of origami in person. Often those sessions prompt discussions about our experiences that have influenced our thinking about artful folding. If you have had the pleasure of attending one of Michael's sessions, perhaps at an origami convention, you'll know what I mean: Michael injects his "LaFossophy" between each instruction as he waits for folders to catch up!

The following are Michael's most useful approaches and productive methods. I have heard him expounding on these topics since I met him in 1988, and I have seen the proof often enough to thoroughly believe in Michael's ideas. They will inspire you.

Preparing Your Heart

Mental preparation for any activity is often the key to a successful and satisfying performance. The right mental attitude allows you to focus on the task at hand. Master Yoshizawa folded with a peaceful spirit, usually composing his thoughts while centering his physical body in a comfortable position for a moment of meditation or prayer. The physical act of closing your eyes, and bringing the palms of your hands together in a way that resembles the posture of prayer is an act of intentional focus. Proper breathing is also important to any performer, and long, deep, conscious breathing pumps oxygen into the brain.

Dancing with the Paper

The process of folding and then turning the paper to reposition it for comfort before the next fold is akin to a dance, and even more so when the paper is large and the maneuvers are performed in the air, rather than against a table surface. The fluidity of motion, and the changing relationships between the paper, the person and the planet is enjoyable for the folder, and entertaining for spectators.

Poems for the Fingers

The simpler, elegant designs in this book can be easily memorized and then performed for pure joy, similar to that from reciting the work of a favorite poet. It is fun to practice the motions, savoring the rhythm while performing such an "origami poem." When Michael "recites" such a piece in front of an audience, they fully understand the joy of the entire creative process.

Giving and Receiving

One need not spend a lot of money on meaningful gifts. Repaying the kindness of a thoughtful gift can be as easy as folding your favorite model. Whenever you receive a gift wrapped with beautiful paper, carefully save the paper. How delighted your friend will be when you cut a square, fold, and present your origami gift of thanks. What better gift can there be than one folded by your own hands from that same, special paper that your friend selected and will be sure to recognize?

Send a personalized "thank you" by folding a model for the gift-giver from the paper used to wrap the original gift.

Finding Joy in Transformation

Origami is a metamorphic art: A sheet of paper is transformed by folding only; nothing is added or removed. This aspect of change is captivating when one contemplates the possibilities and the magnitude

LaFosse's inspired "Goldfish." "It just appeared in my hands." The paper was a gift from Akira Yoshizawa.

of the change, as well as the chosen process. Some models are "action models," which convert from one form to another even after the folding is finished. Shape transformation is captivating, and it is useful when you want to introduce yourself to strangers in a memorable way.

Awakening the Spirit

The final step is to open the eyes! Those of us who fold origami animals know how magical it can be to create an individual with a presence of its own. This makes origami so empowering to young children. They're hooked as soon as you show them how to fold a square into a cute little fox in just five steps! Any origami creature can become their leading character in a new story or tall tale. The models may be pasted in rows to grace the pages of a customized scrapbook or securely mounted as a mobile. The artistic expression and emotions that you fold into your origami creations are unlimited. They may evoke an endearing and cuddly friend or even the most wicked of demons. Master Yoshizawa is said to have folded a mask of a Japanese No Theater character, Hannya, who was so diabolical in appearance that Yoshizawa "burst into uncontrollable tears — and was immediately hospitalized by extreme nervous and mental exhaustion," according to biographer, Leland Stowe ("The Paper Magic Of Origami," *Hawai'i Beacon* magazine, July, 1970). Perhaps some spirits should remain asleep!

Being Open to Inspiration

"I don't feel that I create these. I feel that God guides me. I'm even sur-

prised at what comes out." — Akira Yoshizawa, according to biographer, Leland Stowe, 1970.

Unexplained, inspired art can simply happen. We recall the day Michael was fumbling with an orange square of textured, Leathack paper that Yoshizawa had given to him. Michael was supposed to be working on another project that day, and when I came home from work, he met me standing at the top of the staircase, beaming with joy, with a stunning origami goldfish cradled in the palms of this hands. "I have no idea how to repeat it. I don't even remember doing it. It just appeared in my hands!" he said. It wasn't until several years later that he struggled to rediscover the folding process so he could diagram it for *Advanced Origami* (Tuttle Publishing).

Making Legendary Friends

Many designs have developed personas that become established into pop lore. The traditional Japanese origami crane is the most famous of these celebrated models. The age-old legend of the crane living 1,000 years morphed into a poignant tale of Sadako, a kindergartner battling radiation sickness after the atomic bombing of Hiroshima. The Spanish Pajarita design is yet another example. The tales expand and evolve with repeated telling. These classic designs now enjoy worldwide recognition beyond just origami enthusiasts. The Internet allows new designs to go viral as each story is shared and re-shared. We now see young folders clutching their own Origami Yodas

folded from Tom Angleberger's published tales, *The Strange Case of Origami Yoda*, (Abrams, 2010). These legendary friends need not be simple: At folding conventions, we often see several youngsters comparing their versions of Satoshi Kamiya's "Ancient Dragon."

Legendary zeal happened to one of our students when he was younger. John Scarborough was an inventive creator who had learned to fold several origami animals while attending classes at our Origamido Studio. One day, he appeared with his mom and dad to reveal his own delightful origami composite design that he called the

John Scarborough proudly shows his original "Moxaroo," and the book of its lore.

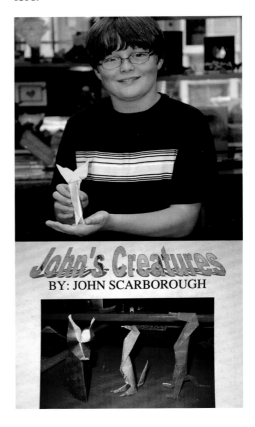

John's Creatures
BY: JOHN SCARBOROUGH

Greg Mudarri's legendary "Crane Riders" in a display diorama.

"Moxaroo." He described it as having the head of a fox, the body of a mouse, and the tail of a kangaroo. With each subsequent meeting, there would be an added model, a tidbit of lore, often accompanying a newly folded version of the Moxaroo, or perhaps its prey. Finally, he presented us with a three-ring binder of the story, complete with life cycle factoids about his mythical creatures. This was a wonderful chapter in his creative origami life that we all still recall with a broad smile.

Our dear friend, coauthor and graphic designer, Greg Mudarri, recalled that as a child he was captivated by a *U.S. News & World Report* illustration from 1987 depicting a businessman riding an origami Japanese Crane folded from a tax form. He designed an origami human figure to nicely fit atop an origami crane. He exhibited a series of "Crane Riders" at our Studio, depicting them gathered around a campfire, capturing and taming the huge, fanciful creatures. Eventually, he designed an origami model to produce both crane and rider from a single, uncut square. In 2013, Greg contacted Ben Luce, the graphic artist who had designed the original illustration, in Los Angeles. A mere 26 years later, Greg met Ben and finally had the chance to thank the man whose artistic efforts inspired him to embark on so many hours of joyful paper folding. Imagine how you too can develop your own lore and legends around your favorite origami creations.

Gifts from Our Mentors

What would we be without the origami designers who have gone before

us? Just as Michael was transformed by seeing the color photos of remarkable origami in the 1970 *Readers Digest* article about Master Yoshizawa and others, the person discovering origami art today is about to embark upon a journey of discovery enhanced by exposure to the works of previous designers, artists, diagrammers, and hand papermakers. While many folders draw inspiration from works by others, one's own work is enough to propel some artists into a frenzy of innovative folding. The topic of one-upsmanship was beautifully illustrated in Vanessa Gould's Peabody-Award-winning origami documentary, *Between the Folds*, in the chapter titled, "The Bug Wars." While she addressed one aspect of technical folding, the same arguments work for spurring one another on artistically as well.

We owe a great debt of gratitude to Mr. & Mrs. Akira Yoshizawa, Samuel & Jean Randlett, Neal Elias, Patricia Crawford, Robert Harbin, Florence Temko, Eric Joisel, Vincente Palacios and many other origami designers and authors who, through their inspiring publications, paved the way for us and new generations of origami designers. We have immense gratitude, love and affection for Elaine and Sidney Koretsky, founders of Carriage House Paper in

Brookline, Massachusetts, who helped us and our students explore the world of hand paper making, from gaining experience with the paper-making plants that they cultivated in their yard, to fiber processing techniques and archival coloring with pigment systems. Their accomplished artist daughter, Donna, now continues their important legacy through Carriage House Paper in Brooklyn, New York.

Our effectiveness as teachers is a credit to the work of Lillian Oppenheimer, and her eclectic collection of designers, presenters and volunteers at origami conventions. As an example, Kyoko and Shigeo Kondo have not only been long-time supporters of OrigamiUSA, they also personally mentor younger folding artists, and have done so ever since we can remember. We have lovingly bestowed upon Kyoko the affectionate moniker "Chairman of the Board" because she constantly urges us to explore new projects, publications and ways to make our living by doing what we love to do. The best way we can thank these selfless mentors is to help grow a new crop of passionate, innovative and talented artists and teachers to willingly share their enthusiasm for artful paper folding with others, well into the future.

Folding Socially
MEET AND FOLD FOR FUN!

If you enjoy playing cards or dancing, you might also like the interplay of folding origami with others. We usually fold with others gathered around a large table when we are preparing special displays or commercial art installations. If there is latitude in the design, such as when composing origami blossoms, stems and leaves, it is fun to gather opinions about what sizes, colors or positions look best. Often somebody will discover a shortcut or tip to make the folding more precise or efficient. We learn about new tools, papers and materials whenever we gather with folding friends. When we take a break from the task at hand, we show each other new origami designs that we have developed, modified or learned.

If you think you might enjoy the company of other origami enthusiasts, visit the website of OrigamiUSA at origamiusa.org to find listings of folding groups in your area.

Continent or Island?
It used to be common for origami artists to work in isolation. There were

Folders of all ages enjoy making origami at this Peabody Essex Museum workshop.

few publications and organizations to support a serious paper folder. It can also be more fun to solve a problem on your own, particularly when it takes intense thought over long periods of time. Designing with little outside influence certainly can produce fresh results. Folders working in isolation have become famous when examples of their innovative work suddenly burst upon the scene. Shocking new techniques advanced by isolated artist certainly make a refreshing splash in the art world.

Today's ubiquitous Internet has made artistic isolation more difficult. New ideas and techniques may instantly pollinate the minds of thousands of contemporary artists. Those who are receptive absorb these lessons and then apply their own spin, often resulting in clever variations.

This change has its pros and cons. At certain points in your career you may prefer isolation, perhaps during the birth of a breakthrough, or when you simply need to find your own voice. The connected crowd produces fairly steady and incremental advancement, and you may draw strength from the inspiration of others' work. Luckily, the choice is yours.

Folding for the World
In any new art, the "pioneers" invariably set the tone for those who follow. Because this "folding as art" is so new, many of the greatest origami designers of all time are alive today, and their signature works may be important from a historical

perspective. Realizing the magnitude of this impact, one designer friend shares only one new design with the folding world each year, and the anticipation within the community of fans is palpable. Other designers seem to want to publish anything they can think of, and then they let the origami community play the part of the critical filter, as they weigh in with praise or critique. As society changes, our collective tastes in art also change, and it is instructive to look back. Good design is timeless, and while an origami creation is no less a product of the time in which it was developed, the artifacts of our civilization are snapshots that teach us about the human mind and the condition of society in that place, and at that instant.

Just Right
"I don't know anything about art, but I know what I like," is an oft-heard comment in art exhibitions. Since the public is essentially without knowledge about origami art, the first time your work is shown in public, it is sure to garner a wide range of reaction. The best strategy is to show the work that you are most comfortable showing, and that process of curating comes down to a simple question: "Is it just right?" Often, you won't be able to put your finger on exactly what is troubling you about a piece of folded art, but you know that there is something that hasn't yet gelled. Don't show it yet. Let it simmer in your mind. Revisit the subject with a clear head. Try a different type of paper, a different size or fold it with some different tools or techniques. This is the fun of exploring origami art as a lifelong passion!

It's All About the Art

GROWTH THROUGH SHARING & CRITIQUE

Michael's "A Rose for Irene," named for Richard Alexander's mother, which was on display at the "Less = More" exhibition at the Honolulu Museum of Art from February to May in 2015.

If you want to fold more artfully, "Get thee to an art museum!" It will help immensely to expose yourself to a wide variety of art. Study it, and enjoy getting to know other artists who love to visit museums and discuss the works. Line, form, relationship, color, light — all of the countless aspects of fine art are considered by artists and revealed in the thousands of works of art gracing the walls of our finest public museums. If your folding attempts are ever to be considered by others as art, you should have certainly first become familiar with the dialogue of art history. Art from ancient civilizations was studied, copied and regurgitated by the artists of subsequent generations in a process that continues to this day, and will repeat throughout time. You are now part of that splendid tradition of building on the achievements of those artists who have said something important about being human. Perhaps you have something new to add about beauty, love or struggle. What do you want to say to the future artists who will someday gaze upon

your masterwork? Michael sums it up by saying, "I believe that art is the unique contribution that any individual can give to their chosen craft. The greatest value of art is realized by the artist, during the journey. The resulting product, or artifact, is another matter, entirely." That dialogue about origami art — what is, and what isn't — will surely go on forever.

Connoisseurship, or Calibrating Your Sense of Quality

Although modern and expressive origami is relatively recent, there is already a rich body of design on every level, from amateur to professional, This provides enjoyable foraging for the origami connoisseur and folded art collector. How does your work stack up? There is no better way to calibrate the quality of your work than to show it at one of the several annual origami conventions now held in at least twenty cities around the globe. "Get thee to an origami convention!" You will see works by your contemporaries, and at every level of complexity and artistic

prowess. Make an effort to meet like-minded folders (There will also be critics who will spare no feelings in telling you what they think of your subjects or technique). We encourage you to engage in spirited discussions about your art. See if you can put your finger on what moves your emotions or impresses you, and what doesn't. Try to carefully articulate the reasons for your opinions. After such healthy discussions, nearly every exhibitor packs up their display table with thoughts of what they will do differently in the future. As Red Sox baseball fans, we grew up fond of saying, "Just wait until next year!"

Avoid Overthinking

If you are susceptible to deadly "overthink," we don't have any advice for you other than "put it down and walk away." There is usually great value in having a fresh look at something you have done before. Sometimes it only takes a day to pass, sometimes a week or even a month may elapse before it becomes obvious that additional changes are needed (or not).

Avoid Overworking Your Art

Overworking is as dangerous as overthinking, and the two often travel hand-in-hand. Overworking a design is one thing; overworking the paper is yet another. Paper is a fragile medium, and it tells you quite quickly when it is overworked — but of course, when it does, it's too late! Folders who moisten their paper must be more careful because the structure of the paper can easily disintegrate if too much water is added and then you provide too much manipulation to that area. My dad

"Balancing Seahorses" by LaFosse, from Alexander's handmade gampi papers. Goal met! Careful folding passes the test when they stand on their own.

provides similar, useful advice about spray painting: "Give it just a gentle kiss with a light spritz, and then walk away! You will be tempted to hit it again, but DON'T DO IT! Just go paint something else while you let it dry."

Finding Your Own Level

Origami can be exciting and interesting at any level of complexity, from single-fold expressions, to highly realistic and detailed modeling. We find that if somebody enjoys the magic of folding paper, then they will tend to fold those things that bring them the most comfort or joy. Some appreciate the social interaction with others more than the physical product itself, and these folders may tend to enjoy "performance origami" and "Story-gami" models, especially when they are working with "pre-folders" (the very young), or "post folders," such as senior citizens or others who may be unable to fold because of arthritis or injury. Such people who would simply rather watch than fold enjoy origami the most as spectators.

At the other end of the spectrum are folders who explore origami as a novel way to challenge themselves to understand or illustrate complex, mathematical concepts, theorems and proofs. They might wonder if they can solve the puzzle presented by an elegant crease pattern or complex diagrams. Perhaps they'll see potential in a particular model for their own modification or interpretation. They simply may be curious about the folding method, or the initial base chosen by the designer.

Somewhere in between those two extremes lies the greater area of the bell curve of folders and crafters who simply enjoy sharing popular favorites, or perhaps recreating the most recently published models. There are organizations with members in all of these categories. If you want to find other people who share your particular interests, visit OrigamiUSA online. They support regional groups of paper folders and may help you participate in local origami activities.

Finding Your Own Voice

Early on, an artist attempts to copy the works of others. Sometimes those works speak to him or her in some special way. The effort is often less than satisfying, and so the journey of the artist is to confront obstacles that may include technical limitations, prejudices and ignorance. One by one, the artist explores approaches and methods that address and resolve each obstacle or impediment. Gaining fluency through persistent effort while striving for facility allows an artist to become most familiar with those methods that feel the most natural, or seem to resonate within. Folding artists will eventually zero-in on a particular style that expresses their "voice," much in the way a singer develops their own unique approach to singing. Finding your voice for the first time is excit-

ing, but it is only the first part of a long journey. Allowing it to evolve as you grow can be even more thrilling.

We know many folding artists who have set high standards for themselves, and have found their voice. Their work is magnificent and easily recognizable.

Making a Model "Sing"

We practice origami to become better folders, but we repeat certain favorite lesons until we can make them "sing." During an exhibition at an origami convention, you may see the work of an artist who consistently produces models that rise above the rest. Each may excel at a particular subject or model, and their mastery is evident. One need not hover around his or her display for long before you hear a visitor say, "Nobody does it better." If the subject is silk tessellations, the name mentioned might be Chris Palmer. If the subject is a gorgeous floral arrangement, expect to hear the name Delrosa Marshall. If the extraordinary display is of origami animals, we might guess the folder is Sipho Mabona or Robert Lang. This predictable, exceptional level of artistry does not happen by accident. It takes an enormous amount of recital time. These artists know how to make their work sing, and we take delight in any of their public performances.

Crystalline Beauty

Some compositions appear unfinished. Others appear overworked. At some point in between, during the process of folding an origami sculpture, a little voice in your head should say, "That gels." The ability to recognize, attain, and more importantly, avoid going beyond that critical point is just one thing that distinguishes an artist from a less experienced folder. We love to see the shoeboxes of works that our students bring to the Studio to show to us. Their technical prowess is often quite evident; it seems to drip off the models, yet the art is not there yet. This is usually a phase that young folders pass through. With coaching, they eventually learn to recognize exactly when there is just enough effort, and not too much.

Overcoming "Folder's Block"

If you are an artist with a vision, you are truly blessed! Writers often suffer from "writer's block," a condition of anxiety felt when the words refuse to appear on the blank page. The same can happen with artists or creative people in any discipline. Sometimes an artist "falls into a rut" — doing only familiar designs with their favorite, familiar materials. Another common complaint we hear is that an artist may have no shortage of vision — things they want to fold or accomplish — but every attempt falls far short of their vision. Some designers describe vivid dreams of folding something that turns out to be impossible when they try to recreate the experience while awake. Others "see" way too much, and they bury themselves in piles of mediocre madness (It may be time for them to take a trip to the paper-recycling center). Whenever you feel stymied or artistically inarticulate, consider the following suggestion:

Gain a New Perspective

The best way that we have found to recharge our reservoir of artistic vision is to change our scene and our routine. Whether we go local or travel to new lands, the effect is refreshing. Our time in Hawai'i was a way to make new friends, experience interesting creatures and recharge our spirits in refreshingly beautiful landscapes. This also provided us with new colors, smells and sounds, and our palette of handmade papers brightened considerably. Grab a pack of paper and just GO SOMEWHERE!

Collaborate

The creative staff in any company needs a shot in the arm once in a while. We have been fortunate to work with several creative staffs at workshops for innovators and with design teams of well-known companies. We have prepared teachers' workshops at schools and colleges, and find that when artists learn a new technique,

they immediately think up many ways to apply it to their art. Just as there are many ways to construct a bridge over a river, bridging your vision into the world of reality as a tangible sculpture requires considerable thought, planning and experimentation. Working with somebody else is synergy at its best, creating together more than the sum of what each could do alone. We believe that those who enjoy that collaborative process become better artists.

Folding for Oneself

That pendulum can swing both ways. Perhaps you need a break from long periods of collaboration. If you are the rare breed of artist with no need of an audience, origami may be a perfect solitary pastime for you. One friend enjoys origami immensely, but only to satisfy her own curiosity. She rarely keeps anything that she folds, and she does not fuss with obtaining fancy papers. To her, the only thing that is important is to understand the structure of the model. Other artists also develop their folding talent for solitary joy. Perhaps they have such high expectations that they are too shy to ever show their work to another human being. Some keep nothing. Others keep all of their work, but they keep it hidden away. Many people fold for relaxation or for escape from worldly matters in the same way that it can be fun to get lost in a novel.

Michael's "Tulip for Betty," named for his mother, on display at the "Less = More" exhibition at the Honolulu Museum of Art from February to May in 2015.

Practical Considerations
MORE TIPS FOR FOLDERS

Considering the question of scale — each model has a fairly well-defined, optimum range of scale that translates to the perfect paper size, or range of preferable sizes. When a model just seems perfect, you know that the artist has chosen the scale wisely. This choice also depends upon the paper thickness for a given model, and it is a mark of an experienced folder when you see those choices perfectly executed. We are also aware of the impressive work that it takes to create examples that fall outside of that usual window or envelope. When you see such works, realize that they probably rely on hidden engineering, support structures, materials, tricks or tools to accomplish the extraordinary. Our display of Origami Japanese Cranes at a pharmaceutical convention required a special, two-piece design, and internal structural supports and clamping devices in order to show off their seven-foot wingspans.

Crease Patterns

Crease patterns are efficient puzzles useful to adept folders, and in a perfect world where there are no beginners and everyone has above average skills, there would be no need for elaborate diagrams, drawings, photos or video instructions. We don't live in that world. Regardless, if you have been folding for a while, it might be fun to practice your proficiency at figuring out crease patterns. Another way to challenge yourself is to use a right-handed crease pattern to create a left-handed origami model (such as Michael's Yellow Tang for Mariko, page 64). This ability to translate "hand-edness," or chirality, is a useful skill that improves with practice. Crease patterns have become an important component of public displays of folded art. When a visitor looks at a piece of origami art without realizing that it was folded from a single square with no cuts, the impact may not be as powerful as it would be if a crease pattern accompanied the work to communicate that added information. The same is true of popular songs. Knowing why a songwriter was moved to create a piece of music often adds immeasurably to the total experience.

Holding Hand, Working Hand

We in New England are mindful of the concept of the "division of labor," especially every time we enjoy eating our tasty, large-claw lobsters from the icy North Atlantic. The local lobsters have two distinct and specialized claws — a smaller and sharper "pincher" claw,

Inside each crane is a wooden fixture to clamp the halves together and support the hanging cable.

LaFosse folds his signature "Origamido Butterfly" from a 5-foot square of purple handmade paper that we made for an episode on German TV.

and a massively powerful "crusher" claw. Think of this animal whenever you fold paper, because one of your hands will be better at holding the paper, and the other will be skilled at placing the creases. "Hold before you fold," is a common reminder we hear from Michael when he is working with a new folder. Printed origami diagrams are to blame for many of a new folder's difficulties. For economy, the diagrams are rarely rotated on the page to show in the actual orientation that we normally use when we are placing a crease. When one sits at a table with the paper before them, the natural position of the fingers points away from the folder's body. That is also the most natural direction for a flap of paper to be moved by those extended fingers — away from the body. This means that the paper will be frequently turned, flipped and repositioned for folding comfort, and the hand that firmly pins the model to the table is the "holding hand" while the fold is being positioned and creased by the "folding hand." Some folders can perform delicate maneuvers only with their dominant hand, and they focus their efforts on that hand. Others strive for equal facility in their hands, and exercise their non-dominant hand as a way to challenge their minds.

Chemical Size

"Size" is common term used to describe a variety of natural and synthetic chemical additives used to harden the surface of the paper, control the absorption of paint and ink, and to stiffen it. Exploring and becom-ing familiar with a new tool or technique can blast open a passageway to exciting possibilities. The unseen workhorse of today's folded paper sculpture is methylcellulose (MC for short), and if you want to become a more artful folder and have not used it, give it a try. This reversible, water-soluble paste allows two thin sheets of paper to be pasted together (back coating). It also helps the paper layers stay put as you narrow (or "skinny") any long, thin appendage, such as an insect's leg or antennae. It also toughens the paper and strengthens the stance, making the piece stable when dried. Yoshizawa and other advanced folders used starch (wheat) paste. Photos of those works published in 1970 inspired Michael to design his own origami and create shaped, folded sculptures. When Michael was a teenager he worked at the Fitchburg Public Library and helped repair books. This made him aware of insect and mold problems associated with starch paste. Sometime in 1973, his father, a building contractor, saw how Michael was trying to back coat two sheets of paper for his origami designs. His dad suggested that Michael try Metylan, a wallpaper paste that he used (which turned out to be MC). It worked great, not only for back coating, but for sculpting or "modeling" his finished works! Unlike starch paste, MC gel did not go bad.

Those who are new to the techniques of back coating and wet folding with methylcellulose may at first be intimidated by using size. However, most of our students experience a remarkable improvement in their work when they wet fold their first sheet of handmade duo paper (laminated with MC gel between).

Research on the Internet

The Internet is now loaded with photos of exceptional models. It can't hurt to search for an image of an origami subject to assess the state of the art. Perhaps you will find that your own vision has not only been done before — but that it has been done much better than you had ever imagined. On the other hand, an Internet search may afford you smooth sailing in uncharted waters, going where no folder has gone before (or if they have, they never returned!) The other side of this coin is that seeing other works will influence your work. Consider the risks.

These were just some of the nuggets that have come up in discussion at the Studio while folding paper with other artists and students interested in more artful folding. We hope that you find some of these ideas or suggestions useful and thought provoking as you explore origami as an expressive art form.

Choosing and Preparing Your Origami Paper
QUALITY CONSIDERATIONS

A selection of handmade abaca papers made at the Origamido Studio.

We fold a wide variety of papers, but lasting art requires quality not commonly found in readily available, decorative papers. Here's what you should know:

Kraft

The most common papers readily available to the folding artist today are made from wood pulp. These are also the least expensive papers because trees (and tree-top scrap remaining from logging operations) are readily available, and trees are a renewable resource. Huge paper mills located in the northern climates continuously receive truckloads of trees, often from mixed species. The wood is chopped in large-scale machinery, and the inch-sized wood bits are soaked in water. The kraft process, a common method to process the wood bits with harsh chemicals (sodium hydroxide and sodium sulfide), was developed in Germany over a century ago. Since this treatment yields fiber that is strong enough for most general-purpose papers, it was given the name "kraft," which means "strength" in German. The alkaline solution and wood mixture is cooked under high pressure with steam. This process quickly separates the brown, gooey, unwanted lignins from the desired fibers of cellulose. Today, that stock is often mixed with fiber from post-consumer paper recycling. You are probably most familiar with the sturdy brown paper grocery bags produced by the kraft process. When similar material is corrugated and laminated between layers to hold the ribs in place, it forms cardboard for boxes and packaging.

Fiberboard for shoeboxes and cereal boxes are yet another familiar, less-refined kraft product.

Bond

Long ago, the loose fuzz on minimally processed kraft papers interfered with ink pen nibs, and so those loose fibers needed to be "bound" onto a smooth, flat surface to produce reliably acceptable stock. This is why writing paper is called "bond." That same fuzz also affects the performance of mechanical copiers and printing machines today, and so copier paper is now often called "office bond." Additional refinement is needed to produce fine writing papers. The pulp is usually bleached white to improve writing legibility, and then the surface is made harder and more opaque by adding minerals such as kaolin clay or chemical "size," such as polymers that harden when the pulp is dried or heated. Bond papers tradition-

ally folded quite nicely, but now manufacturers seem to be incorporating more recycled, waste fiber "streams." Commercial bond stock is usually not considered a permanent media for folded art due to the variable and unknown origin of recycled content.

Bond papers do work well for practice, especially if the models have only a few steps, and for folding any models not intended to last for posterity. Such machine-made paper will yield acceptable, six-inch, Japanese origami cranes. As you will learn in the Japanese Crane lesson (page 34), a beginning folder may soon notice that the points of the beak, wings and tail are more difficult to form perfectly from bond paper, especially on one side of each corner. Part of this is due to the relative thickness, but most of the problem comes from the grain, or disproportionate alignment of fibers. A crease formed between fiber strands is easier to make than one placed perpendicularly across the ends of aligned fibers. Placing creases to form an "airplane point" at one of a square's corners tends to be more difficult on one side, where the fiber alignment opposes the direction of the intended fold as the adjacent edges are brought together. One flap will easily bend because the crease is being made parallel to, or with the grain; but the other flap resists, with the alignment of the fibers forcing the actual crease to splay away from the corner. Michael likes to use a tool to "convince" the ends of the fibers (cut across the grain) to fold where he wants them to, rather than splay away.

To counteract this tendency, most types of office bond can be "zone folded," by applying a localized swipe of moisture along the intended fold line with a cotton swab (whereas "wet folding," or moistening the entire sheet, usually causes puckering of the model as it dries). The thickness of bond paper helps the beginning folder learn to anticipate accommodating the buildup of multiple layers by leaving a slight gap between raw edges as the crease is placed. This allows sufficient room for them to come together as those edges are folded inside subsequent folds.

Origami Paper

Also called "kami," which is Japanese for paper, "origami paper" is a term that many folders today use to describe the ubiquitous packaged folding papers made from thinner sheets of wood pulp. It typically has color applied to only one side. Kami was developed in the 1800s to support the paper folding exercises introduced to young children attending Friedrich Froebel's Kindergarten. In the United States, Milton Bradley, a lithographer, produced some of the first widely distributed, commercially packaged materials designed to support the newly imported Kindergarten system. We credit Froebel with insisting upon "one sheet, no cuts," and the use of small squares ("to better fit small hands") with color on only one side. These were selected for economy as well as for the interesting patterns produced when the paper is folded in particular ways. "Duo kami" (two-colored origami paper) describes folding paper with two colors — one on each side of the paper.

Momigami

"Momigami" refers to Japanese papers with decorative, crinkled or wrinkled surfaces. There are several modern methods to mass-produce imitation momigami from wood pulp papers.

Long-time folders pine for the days when regular origami paper was much stronger than it is today. They've noticed the drop in quality through the last few decades, probably due to the inclusion of post-consumer waste paper from offices, factories and households. This discarded packaging, junk mail, newspapers and magazine fiber stock is highly variable from time to time, and from location to location. The inclusion of recycled stock generally shortens the average length of the cellulose fibers in the mix, and so other, longer, stronger fibers or polymers must be added to the batch to boost its strength.

Mass production economy dictates that wood pulps must be processed quickly, and that is most easily accomplished with aggressive chemicals such as strongly alkaline solutions, which are neutralized with correspondingly strong acids. Even though

Origami paper and foils are inexpensive and widely available in wonderful patterns and colors that make these papers so popular with folders.

Commercially available art papers can yield satisfactory results. They are a step up from cheap "origami papers," but not as prized as handmade papers.

this stock is thoroughly rinsed, traces of acid can and do remain in the paper (called internal, or residual acids). Batch variability makes it difficult for the consumer to know exactly what is contained within inexpensive papers. Rapid, global industrialization has also increased coal burning and the amount of acidic compounds of chlorine, sulphur and nitrogen in the atmosphere. Over long periods of time, papers without a sufficient level of internal buffering can discolor, fade, turn yellow and / or become brittle with age. Although some paper makers add alkaline buffering compounds to counteract this effect, doing so adds expense and changes the nature of the paper.

Because of this, there are several brands of papers used by commercial and fine artists that have become popular with paper folders. We don't know exactly what is in each of these materials because paper formulas are often considered trade secrets, but there seems to be a higher level of quality control with the following brands of so-called "art papers."

Art Papers

These are a commercially available compromise. They are more expensive than bond, but still affordable, and often sold as "archival." As folding materials, these do work well for many wet-folded objects. These papers are available in different weights, and so the relative thickness of the thin-ner weights is usually not a problem when used to fold larger models for public display. Because these papers are designed for artistic uses, origami displays in retail store windows look great when the subjects are wet folded with these popular brands: Zanders' "Elephant Hide"; Samwha Paper Co.'s "Leathack" and "Tant"; Graphic Products Corporation's "Wyndstone"; Daler Rowney's "Canford"; and Canson's "Mi-Teintes." These are just some of the popular brands of strong art paper favored by well-known origami artists such as Chris Palmer, who tessellates large sheets; or Robert Lang, who wet folds structurally strong bowls, goblets and boxes. We have many pieces of art folded from these commercial products by artist friends through the years. Unfortunately, we have found that the colors of these commercially available "art papers" tend to fade when the objects are exposed to bright light (on display in the gallery, or exposed to sunlight).

If you enjoy the folding qualities of art papers, we recommend that you consider first coloring the surface with an acrylic wash or pigmented paint similar in tone to the paper itself.

In general, wood pulp paper is usually not the best choice when folding art that you might want to outlast you — perhaps your heirs (or the museum that they sell it to) will want it to be around for hundreds of years without any serious compromises in strength or any changes in color.

Watercolor Paper

Other high quality, commercially produced papers made from exceptionally strong fibers have been used by fine artists for hundreds of years for charcoal sketching, pencil and ink pen drawing, and for painting. The most common paper choice for these fine art uses is fairly thick watercolor paper made of cotton. This material also works well for folding larger works of origami, but it usually proves too thick for the majority of origami subjects. Because it is also highly sized, it will require moistening before folding to prevent cracking. Many folders are inexperienced with wet-folding techniques, and so they often over-wet the paper, which can result in puckering when it is dried.

We make more paper than we can use, so we bring the excess to the paperfolding conventions we attend.

US Money, or Paper Currency

US dollars are made from a combination of fibers specifically selected for durability, and therefore we feel that they belong in this category as a superior material for paper folders.

Handmade Papers

A piece of folded art is more likely to last when it is folded from high grade cellulose harvested from superior plants, at the right time in the season, and carefully processed in the correct manner by an experienced paper maker. Handmade papers with exceptionally high strength can be made from natural plant fibers of abaca (in the banana family of monocotyledons), kozo (paper mulberry), hemp, cotton, flax or gampi, or blends of any of these. These are what we use when we make handmade papers at the Origamido Studio. These plants produce fibers that are usually more supple and longer, and so they generally do not require chemical binders, size and other additives to impart strength to the sheet, affording a better resistance to aging and embrittlement. We use the Aardvark system of pigmenting the fibers (after the fibers are beaten) to minimize discoloration. Many commercial papers are dyed with inexpensive chemicals that fade when exposed to sunlight.

Skins, Hides, and Other Collagen Papers

Parchments (sheepskin) and vellums (other animal skins) and even synthetic faux parchments or faux vellums represent a class of disparate modern engineered materials that the paper artist should evaluate on a case-by-case basis. Any skin-based folding materials were historically preserved with inorganic toxins, such as chromium (still commonly used in tanning), but also arsenic, lead or cadmium, added to poison microbes and render the material biologically stable, or "archival." It is difficult to ascertain sufficient safety information about some materials available on the global market, so let the buyer beware. We are always on the lookout for new synthetic substitutes for paper. Most of the innovation seems to be directed toward developing archival materials.

Metals, Foils, and Metallized Films

Florist foils, kitchen foil, kraft paper-backed foils, and the heavier duo foils (often called Japanese foils) are fun to fold because they make attractive objects that are easily shaped. As art materials, they rarely look good after a few years, losing their shine to a visible film of dust or oxidation, or exhibiting signs of crazing (cracking) at the folds that reveals white cellulose substrate.

Plasticized Papers

These include papers with synthetic coatings, including LASER-etched holographics, Mylar colorful wrapping papers, printed wrappers for candy and snacks and specialty foilized composites. They are suitable for short-term commercial uses because of their attractive surface. These plastic components can degrade over time, sometimes flaking, often springing out of shape.

If you desire hybrid properties, you may also want to experiment with laminated composites of pairs of the above, back coated or bonded with methylcellulose, starch paste or even spray or dry mount polymer adhesives.

A palette of colors made for Michael's exhibit at the Morikami Museum & Japanese Gardens, Delray Beach, FL.

Origami Preservation

CREATE THE RIGHT CONDITIONS FOR LONGEVITY

BY ORIGAMIDO STUDIO COFOUNDER RICHARD L. ALEXANDER

Living plants make many different types of cellulose fibers. These versatile polymerized chains of simple sugars can be "assembled" by the plant's cells to be as loose and airy as a cotton ball, or so durable and dense that we use it as hardwood flooring. It may be as moist, supple, flexible and young as a blade of newly formed grass, or it may be tightly compressed by centuries of growth above it, as in the rigid trunk of a giant sequoia tree. Because plant cellulose is of biological origin, paper exposed to the elements will eventually decay, as any dead plant would. The rate of decay depends upon many factors, including time, temperature, moisture, sunlight and the presence of *biota* (microbes such as yeast) capable of utilizing the cellulose as an energy source.

When we make paper, not only can we choose to start with different types of cellulose, we can also process it using a wide variety of techniques, and so the resulting papers can be strikingly different. If you want to preserve your folded art, it helps to know what type of cellulose was used, how the pulp was processed, and how the paper was made. Some papermakers ferment the harvested plant materials first, to biologically digest the protoplasm. Most papermakers use chemicals and heat to digest unwanted parts of the plant. Either method also softens the remaining cellulose fibers. We previously described the kraft process, when pulps are treated with strong chemicals, primarily to remove the lignin. Any residual acidic compounds may continue to attack the cellulose structure over long periods of time if the paper fiber matrix does not contain buffering salts to counteract this reaction.

Assuming that you have folded your work from acid-free, archival, art-quality fibers that have been colored with stable inorganic pigment, your origami sculptures probably need little care to protect them from the big four enemies of paper: excessive moisture, bright light, critters and fire.

HUMIDITY: Most of the larger, professionally managed museums keep their paper works of art in an air-conditioned space set to 68 degrees Fahrenheit, and 50% relative humidity. Digital thermometers that also indicate the relative humidity are now readily available in large department stores. Some of them indicate the highest and lowest values (both for temperature and for relative humidity) during the previous day. This is helpful if you want to determine if you may have a problem in your intended storage area. When the humidity level is lower than 20% most papers become more brittle, which puts them at risk of cracking.

Your climate may require special storage precautions, perhaps only during certain seasons of the year. In general, rooms with regular water use (bathrooms, kitchens, basements, and laundry rooms) are not ideal for storing paper art. Attics experience large swings in temperature and humidity. The best place to store your art when it is not on display is usually in a linen closet or clothing chest. However, cedar wood with aromatic natural oils is used for clothing storage chests because those oils infuse the contents with a fresh fragrance. This fragrance also discourages some insects, but most organic volatile compounds (that our noses detect as fragrance) are also reactive chemicals that can promote unwanted chemical changes the paper. Acid-free photo storage boxes and "museum boxes" are considered best for storing your origami art. If your storage area has any chance of wide swings in humidity, we suggest wrapping the object in archival tissue, and then sealing it in a zipper-type freezer bag. This also allows you to trap

"Portrait of a Friend" and other framed pieces are kept in a room with low humidity.

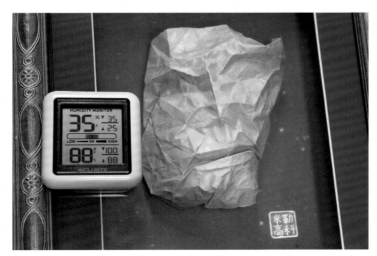

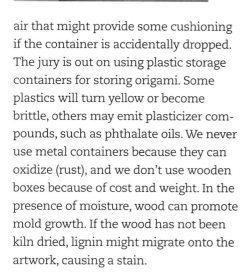

Faded origami lobster (left) shown against a fresh piece of the same Leathack paper. Marbled paper laminate (below) back coated with starch paste, shows "foxing."

Proper care: "Wilbur the Piglet," wrapped in archival tissue, with data label in a labeled archival cardboard box.

air that might provide some cushioning if the container is accidentally dropped. The jury is out on using plastic storage containers for storing origami. Some plastics will turn yellow or become brittle, others may emit plasticizer compounds, such as phthalate oils. We never use metal containers because they can oxidize (rust), and we don't use wooden boxes because of cost and weight. In the presence of moisture, wood can promote mold growth. If the wood has not been kiln dried, lignin might migrate onto the artwork, causing a stain.

BRIGHT LIGHT: Direct sunlight consists of radiation that reacts with, and changes the chemistry of many inexpensive organic dye molecules. Some but not all of the most stable pigments are highly toxic (such as lead and cadmium salts), and so artists compromise to select less toxic, but less permanent, alternatives for bright reds, yellows and greens. Today, unless the pigments are white and brown, it is safe to assume that even the most colorfast pigment systems might contain ingredients subject to at least some fading during prolonged exposure to bright light. The most colorfast pigments are actually ground bits of rock found on the earth's surface. They are chemically stabile precisely because they have been exposed to the elements of sun, wind and rain for thousands (perhaps millions) of years. The pigment system that artists have developed through the centuries (and that we still use today) mostly takes advantage of stable, ground minerals and chemical oxides (such as brown iron oxides and white titanium oxides); if your folded work is pigmented, there is little need to worry about sunlight.

CRITTERS: Art appraisal TV shows have been popular for decades, and the value of a piece of art is largely based upon the quality and condition of the object. Etchings and prints that have been passed through generations often appear on these shows, and are sometimes appraised for a fraction of their potential value because of "foxing." This is a general term referring to discoloration of paper, which can be caused by microbial growth. Storage must exclude insects and mice for obvious reasons, but don't forget the critters too small to see.

MOISTURE: Foxing often indicates that excessive moisture was present at some time. Tree bark contains iron from wind-blown dirt, as well as iron that entered with water through capillary action. Any iron present in the cellulose can oxidize (rust) in the paper. Moisture can also allow fungal growth, and the products of microbial metabolism can produce a visual change, if not a dramatic physical degradation of the strength of the paper. But don't be so overly concerned about this that you soak everything in poison!

FIRE: Paper burns! Keep your precious collection away from stoves, furnaces, electrical equipment and the like.

Fires, critters and floods have robbed us of the historical artifacts of origami art simply because so few pieces have survived more than fifty years. Hopefully, better knowledge about origami art storage will help to preserve what we have for future generations.

In summary, protect your art by using a sturdy archival box designed to store photos or artwork. Store the boxes in a closet within the living space of your home. Add a note with all of the pertinent information about the model: designer, material, size, dates, source of the instructions, etc.; this information will tend to escape your memory.

Showing Your Origami Pieces in Public

SHARE YOUR ART WITH THE WORLD

Artful folders are proud of their work. Showing it in public galleries, museums, libraries and other venues is not only exciting; it permits the necessary critique and discourse so important to the advancement of any art. Don't be selfish; showing your best origami artwork in public is good for you, as well as for the art!

Each opportunity to show your exquisitely folded works in public certainly requires plenty of thought and planning. The world of sculpture can be thought of as a huge pyramid of works piled up according to quality. That pyramid is broad at the base, crowded with mediocre works commonly seen and easily done. As one's gaze ascends the pyramid, the works above are fewer and more exquisite, and they share common attributes. Here, there is obvious evidence of the artists' special attention to poise, balance and proportion. Above, are those equally well executed, but also displaying the artist's masterful command of materials. At the top of the pyramid are the few that are brilliant, captivating, timeless, and perfect. For each, there was no other solution. Society holds onto such high quality works more tenaciously, and we say that the oldest surviving art works have "passed the test of time." Why would any collector want anything less? Museums clamber for this top tier of quality, and so they

compete to discover worthy items as soon as they appear. They won't even know about your work until you make it known. It is important for artists to show their work!

When you have decided to display your folded art in public, consider the best way to present it. The gallery owner or curator may assign your work to a specific location, but often, they will leave it up to you. Laying out a map of the room or gallery will allow you to play with the effect of positioning each display piece within an exhibit.

Consider Relationships

When displaying origami art, we love to explore the aspect of relationships. One piece of origami sitting on its own pedestal may look just fine, and yet it can become stunning, and take on a totally different meaning when shown with another object in a way that communicates a special relationship. The 1797 text on folding variations of the Japanese Origami Crane, *Senbazuru Orikata*, shows a

large crane and a small crane connected at their beaks. This composition is called "Ehiroi, Oya Ko," Japanese for "Parent and Child," and has been a favorite for hundreds of years. Another depiction of a powerful relationship from the same book shows two cranes of equal size, connected at one wing, and it is called, "Imoseyama," or "Sisters." Michael too, is fond of displaying his natural history origami works in pairs, such as butterflies cavorting together or in family groups (easily depicted by folding the parents from larger squares), or perhaps showing two creatures locked in a pose showing their natural predator-prey relationship. These were popular in his origami art show at the Arizona-Sonora Desert Museum in Tucson.

Try larger or smaller pedestals to see what impact your choice makes. If the piece is to be framed for the

Below left: "Ehiroi, Oya Ko" ("Parent and Child"). Below right: Predator and prey — Praying Mantis and Butterfly.

Origami on display at the Honolulu Museum of Art — Spalding House, 2015.

wall, try different backgrounds of different colors. The special limits of origami also provide unique challenges to the folding artist to present the piece in a way that takes best advantage of interesting and appealing lines, angles, facets, shadows and shading. Other spaces and forms will be created by the placement of the work, which defines negative space that should also be considered. Notice how the composition changes with the views, and arrange your exhibit to present the vantage points that you consider the most potent and attractive.

Placement and Sequence

The viewer's opinion of each piece will also be impacted by the context of the placement. Consider what might be near it, and provide a setting that relates to the entire experience. Simpler, yet elegant pieces are often placed to set the stage before complex works are presented. Be careful, though: Truly spectacular pieces can suck the life out of lesser pieces placed around it. Consider isolating the most stunning piece to separate locations if you do not want previously experienced works to color or contaminate the enjoyment of an outstanding piece. At the "Contemporary Origami" art exhibition at the Fitchburg Art Museum, one room held all of the framed pieces of Michael's origami renditions of his

wildlife subjects, while the bold and colorful modular compositions were presented in a separate room across the hall. Walking through an origami exhibition is like participating in a wine tasting event. Have a cracker and a sip of water to cleanse the palate before experiencing a different type of grape!

Lighting

The show's success relies not only on the placement, freshness and quality of the art, but also on skillful lighting. Photographers hired to capture the works for printed posters and catalogs will often spend an entire day composing the best angle of view, background and lighting for the perfect image of an origami masterwork.

Live Viewing Versus the Internet

How many times have you heard a folder at an origami exhibit say, "It looked so much better in the photograph. Reality doesn't do it justice!" The one who controls the image has the power, which is why Internet images of origami art have proliferated,

and their popularity now dwarfs the number of actual visits to exhibitions of original folded works at public venues. Still, we believe that there is no substitute for seeing or experiencing original art directly, and that the process of folding an origami work is also enjoyable and entertaining.

Many museums do not pay stipends to living artists, but they can offer to pay the insurance and shipping costs of borrowed works. Some institutions may also cover the costs of travel for the artist to assist with setting up the show, since folded art sometimes needs post-transit tweaking, or even to attend a gala opening. We often use such a visit as an opportunity to offer a demonstration, workshop or book signing. Sometimes there are funds available for educational programs.

Selling Your Origami Art

TRANSFORM CREATIVITY INTO CASH

BY ORIGAMIDO STUDIO COFOUNDER RICHARD L. ALEXANDER

Museums, as well as corporate and private buyers do purchase and collect folded art. Because origami art is in its infancy, and because several important advancements have been made by living origami artists, some of their works are highly collectable. As Michael has said, "I believe that art is the unique contribution that any individual can give to their chosen craft."

Who is Buying?

Most of the private origami art collectors at this time are also folders who are excited to purchase works by the contemporary artists they admire. If you are an origami artist and want to sell your own expressive works, this discussion is meant to encourage you to proceed, but with some caution.

What is Selling?

We sell only works folded from Origamido handmade paper. With the exception of white watercolor cotton paper, we do not consider commercial papers to be archival. Nearly all of the pieces that we have sold are original designs folded by the creator / artist. We sell many more pieces mounted in deep wall frames (shadow boxes) than pedestal pieces. About half of the art that we sell is commissioned for a special occasion, such as a wedding or

LaFosse's "Flaxen Grackle," protected by mounting in a deep frame, appeals to more buyers than if offered unframed.

retirement gift. This adds the pressure of making several decisions about papers, colors, sizes, frames, poses… (and a deadline), so we prefer to make what we like and then sell our art "off the wall."

Intellectual Property

For centuries, origami was just a craft. The most famous early example of a "how-to" origami book is *Senbazuru Orikata*, published first in 1797 in Japan. It offers instructions for making variations of the still-popular origami crane. The placement of each crease is straightforward, and when anyone followed the published diagrams to reproduce objects, they all looked essentially the same. With such a long history of people sharing their methods, folding and selling multiple copies of anonymously designed "traditional" paper crafts has created a problem for today's expressive origami artists. At some point, the line between craft and art is crossed. Any artist may rightly feel infringed upon when others produce and sell copies of his or her original designs without first obtaining permission, which may include a license, with or without financial compensation. That line may seem fuzzy to the public, especially when so many origami designers publish instructions for others to replicate their creations.

There is an important relationship that exists between a creator and the other folders of his or her work. The lens that brings this relationship into focus is the copyright statement in the instructions (book, video or kit). As designers of original origami, we want anybody to freely enjoy the wonderful process of folding any of our designs for their personal enjoyment. Commercial use (selling objects or images of a designer's works by anyone except the designer) is prohibited, unless and until the designer grants explicit written permission.

As with any expressive art, most origami artists never

The late Eric Joisel organized a showing of remarkable folded artworks at the Carrousel du Louvre in 1998.

grant such permission to others. This longstanding policy certainly extends to our own Origamido Studio: I do not fold any of Michael's designs for sale, nor he mine, without clearly stating so. For example, we co-folded a piece, called "Snap," our second American Alligator, and this fact is clearly displayed on all of the printed attributions. We co-folded that model simply because each alligator takes us fifty hours of folding!

Unfortunately for artists and creators, the Internet has made a lawless Wild West of their intellectual property as portions of songs are "sampled," and visual images are "shared." Such use without the artist's permission constitutes theft. The argument about where to draw the blurred line is sure to continue, but this erosion of intellectual property rights has had a disastrous impact on several of our brilliant origami-designing friends, some of whom have refused to ever publish again. We believe that the original artist must be allowed to control all uses of their own intellectual property, and that nobody should capitalize on the sale of even derivative works without the knowledge, consent and fair remuneration of the original artist. We believe that when somebody sees an original work of folded art offered for sale, the buyer should be able to safely assume that it was made by the hands of the original designer / artist.

There are origami-proficient fans of artful folders who somehow expect to be able to reproduce the works of a master and then put them up for sale. Imagine if Rembrandt or da Vinci produced paint-by-numbers kits for anybody to reproduce their masterworks! The technology of zoom-in video, and even "no-hands" 3-D animated tutorials enables artists to share much more information about how they shape their wet-folded creations artfully.

When professional musicians perform the works of a composer, they pay for that privilege. Our publisher pays us for the right to commercially reproduce and sell our intellectual property. When others unlawfully reproduce our work without such an arrangement it hurts our publisher's sales, our commission and the value of our next book to the next publisher. Without a certain amount of financial success, no designer or artist can continue to share their new designs with the public.

Michael's *Origamido: Masterworks in Folded Paper* (2000, Rockport Publishing) was the first book (that we know of) about origami art, presented essentially without instructions for reproducing the depicted works. Even so, the publisher was reluctant to take the plunge fully, and asked Michael to include a handful of diagrams so the reader could better appreciate what went into the works gracing the full color "coffee-table book" of full-page images. Many of the works depicted in this book were shown to the public at a 1998 exhibition at the Carrousel du Louvre in Paris, France. This exhibition, organized by the late Eric Joisel, had run low on funds before a show catalog could be produced, and Rockport's editors liked Michael's idea of collecting images from fellow exhibitors for a reference work on the state of origami today.

Since origami artists take two-dimensional paper and convert it into three-dimensional sculptures, collecting it does require proper display and storage space. Artists and collectors alike often also possess huge collections of electronic images of works that they have seen at gatherings and conventions. These reside in digital files, since few could ever afford to purchase or display the actual pieces properly. The origami museum of the future probably exists now, albeit spread across disparate electronic collections on the Internet.

Above: LaFosse finishes a bouquet of "Wedding Orchids" for a special bride.

Right: Honolulu paper maker Allison Roscoe joyfully displays a freshly made sheet of premium abaca paper.

Value and Authenticity

As with any artwork, quality is the most important criteria used to establish value. Is the work folded of archival paper colored with fine art quality pigments? The documentation of the provenance of the piece, and the history of its creator, also impact the price. The fact that the methods and materials are available to the public also opens the unfortunate possibility of forgery. It is also important for the artist to stamp or sign and date a work intended for sale. At least for now, it is most common for collectors to become good friends of the artist producing works for their collection. We also videotape the process when we fold many of the works being sold in our gallery, which is another way of providing authenticity to the buyer. Michael began publishing his designs in 1984, and to date, he has contributed to more than eighty publications, so many of his signature pieces are well

documented in those books. Photographs taken at public exhibitions and origami conventions augment the published history of Michael's artistry.

To Sell, or Not to Sell...

You must be comfortable parting with your object. Yoshizawa said that he never sold a single piece because he considered them his children, whom one does not sell, and so he rented them out for advertising photography. One does not live forever, and if you do not sell your works, there will come a time when it might at least make sense to prescribe who should care for your treasures after you have passed. Will your life's work burden your loved ones? Should you have sold them to the highest bidder, or to someone who could provide the best care?

Pricing

Students ask what they should charge for an original work. There are several ways to value art. First, we not only account for the costs of the time and materials, but also account for at least some the time invested in learning the craft and refining that specific design. The quality of the materials should impact the price. Small pieces are expected to cost less, even though any accomplished folder will tell you that they require more skill, finesse, time and patience. Large pieces are much more expensive to frame, and they require more "real estate" (wall space or pedestal space) for proper display, which limits the market to some extent. We would never sell a piece of our work as fine art if it were not folded from archival, fine-art quality materials that I am confident will last as long as any other work of fine art. This is the primary reason that we make our own papers from the finest fibers and pigments. While such handmade paper may cost ten times as much as commercial "artist paper," it only adds a 2% to the price of a $1,000 sculpture. In a couple of decades, the difference between the two will be obvious. Second, as with any other market economy, the laws of supply and demand preside. How many of a particular object do you ever intend, or even want to fold? For our 50-hour American Alligator, the answer is simple: Two. Third, consider provenance. Certainly we charge more for any original pieces that have appeared in publications or exhibitions than we do for other examples. We also remind our students and colleagues that the origami art industry is still very young, and so prices will fluctuate wildly. The bottom line is that the agreed price must satisfy both parties, not only at the time of the transaction, but many years later.

Other Costs

When we fold models for commercial use, we sometimes fold pieces designed by others (with their permission, of course) especially when their design royalty fee is less than the cost for us to design an original alternative. We similarly authorize others to fold and sell origami works designed by us, and as a general rule, the written agreement typically includes a five percent design royalty to us. The design itself is worth something, and that should be part of your price. If you are selling through an art gallery, expect them to mark up your cost by 100 percent to cover their time, overhead (insurance, rent and promotional expenses), and so that becomes part of your price too. Do not forget taxes. Any of your income will be shared with the government, and so if you have your eye on something you want to purchase with the income from an art sale, be sure you are considering net (after taxes) income.

Intangible Rewards

Most purchasers of major works from our gallery are museums, and we are always delighted when a piece of our work is acquired for public appreciation. Our most recent show as of this writing was a display of origami flowers for the Honolulu Museum of Art at their Spalding House facility in Makiki Heights, a neighborhood of Honolulu, Hawai'i. This display was Michael's vision, and he designed each of the pieces (albeit with my hand in the Ohana Orchid plant and his Plumeria). Some museums keep the art for future events and shows. Some facilities, such as the Arizona-Sonora Desert Museum in Tucson (and the Honolulu Museum of Art) do opt to sell some of their works by contemporary artists in order to raise funds to support upcoming artist-in-residencies.

Before our last trip to Honolulu, Michael and I were contacted by an accomplished hand papermaker, Allison Roscoe. She is the resident papermaker at the Honolulu Museum of Art — Spalding House. Rather than build our exhibit in Massachusetts (and then worry about what might happen

when it was shipped to Hawai'i), we decided to travel there to make some of the paper there and fold it on site. At the museum, we had the pleasure of working with Allison and several other local artists. We also held folding workshops, and a hand paper making workshop, together with Allison, so that other budding origami artists could meet her and try their hand at making custom, high-strength, (and exceedingly thin) abaca paper. We back coated, trimmed, folded, and assembled the art for display, right in front of visitors. For ten days in January, when our friends back home were coping with a long and bitter New England winter, we were basking in the beauty, warmth and fragrance of Honolulu! Re-connecting with our old friends and relatives, making new friends, and working with an accomplished colleague such as Allison made our visit delightful. Such intangible considerations might also figure into the price of your art.

Alexander and LaFosse build their display of origami flowers for "Less = More," Honolulu, 2015.

Achieving Elegance in Your Folded Art

Artful folders primarily strive to achieve elegance, which can be difficult to define.

We like to consider three aspects important to achieving elegance in origami art.

1) First, you must be genuinely interested in your subject AND sufficiently motivated to strive for improvement. Inexperienced folders tend to be "checklist" folders. They lack genuine interest and so rarely fold artfully. Study other works that contain elements you admire. Envision something better than what exists. Pre-evaluate the process needed to achieve the desired goal.

2) Practice how to best attain that goal. As one learns to write beautifully in cursive, we begin by thinking about each motion of the hand, but when we carefully train and rehearse our arm, hand and finger muscles to write something as familiar as our own name, the execution will only become fluid when the process becomes automatic. So too can an origami model be practiced until the folding process becomes a reflex. Tools and materials can and do play an important part, but in untrained hands, even the finest tools and materials mean nothing.

3) Incorporate post-folding evaluation and critique. The best artists step back and look at the result. If their eye is well trained to critique their own works, they will be able to identify what they want to change the next time they fold the model in order to improve it. An honest and trusted friend or mentor can help.

Today's super-complex origami designers dazzle their fans at paper folding conventions, but elegance in origami is not related to the complexity of the design or to the number of folds. Viewers are often impressed with elegant origami sculptures that sport hundreds or even thousands of folds, but while technically dazzling, we consider few of the most complex designs as truly elegant. While many single-fold origami sculptures are elegant in their simplicity, it is also easy to make a one-fold paper sculpture that most would consider inelegant. Michael's elegant American Alligator (featured in our book, *Origami Art*, Tuttle Publishing) took us fifty hours of folding, which was difficult and time-consuming, but not complex. Artful folders must build folding skills, but a well-chosen lesson

may hone a technique more efficiently. Why continuously repeat an entire symphony when you only struggle with a certain arpeggio? Conversely, until you master that riff, it must be disappointing to the audience to hear you muck up the same lick every time you attempt that symphony!

Folding skillfully does require practice. Mastery can take years (which makes origami a perfect life-long pursuit), but elegance in origami may have nothing to do with the time it takes to fold a subject.

Some think that elegance is a quality imparted by the paper. Young folders who insist on obtaining some of our "miraculous" custom handmade paper continually clamor for more (apparently forgetting what the word "custom" means). Beautiful paper

certainly adds to the visual experience in the gallery, because human beings are visual creatures that perceive color, textures and patterns. An artist's choice of materials can clearly be an important part of the mix needed to achieve elegance in a piece of origami art. Bear in mind that many a golden flute has made an awful noise in untrained hands, but if that marvelous instrument inspires the student to practice more, well then, perhaps the paper is important after all!

As you work your way through the lessons in this book, the elegance of each design should emerge a little bit more each time you repeat it. Your skills and sensibilities will also develop by repeating these études, and when you tackle an inspired design with

your expert craftsmanship and an informed choice of materials, everything will gel, and you will be hailed as an artful folder. Enjoy the journey!

Elegance is achieved when practiced hands mold fine paper into expressive art.

Your choice of paper can have a major impact on the expressive quality of your finished pieces. The right choice can mean the difference between a clunky practice piece or an elegant work of art.

A Guide to Origami Diagrams and Symbols

Here is a basic guide to the diagrams and symbols used to show how the origami models are to be folded. These may look complicated — but they're not! Spend a little time familiarizing yourself with the symbols to understand what they mean. Once you get the hang of it, the symbols are actually very easy to understand.

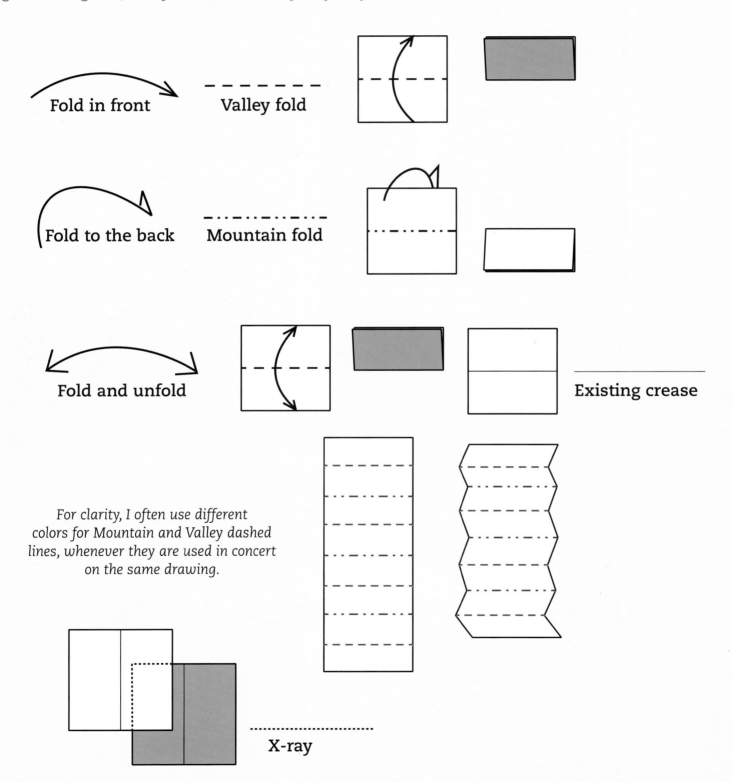

Fold in front

Valley fold

Fold to the back

Mountain fold

Fold and unfold

Existing crease

For clarity, I often use different colors for Mountain and Valley dashed lines, whenever they are used in concert on the same drawing.

X-ray

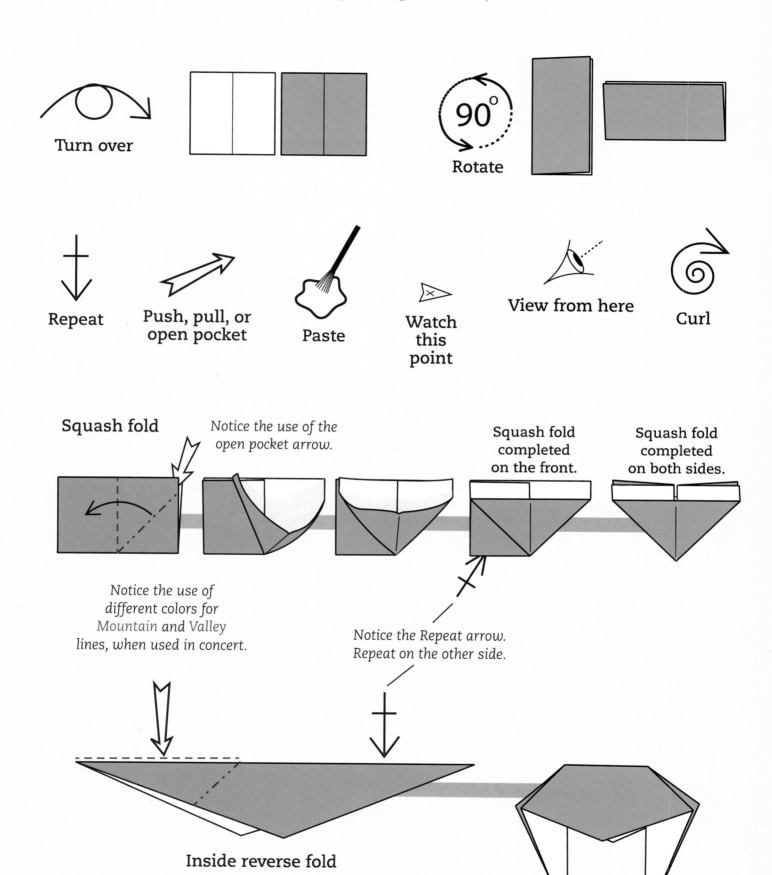

Turn over

Rotate

Repeat

Push, pull, or
open pocket

Paste

Watch
this
point

View from here

Curl

Squash fold

Notice the use of the
open pocket arrow.

Squash fold
completed
on the front.

Squash fold
completed
on both sides.

Notice the use of
different colors for
Mountain and Valley
lines, when used in concert.

Notice the Repeat arrow.
Repeat on the other side.

Inside reverse fold

THE PROJECTS

The Japanese Crane

traditional design

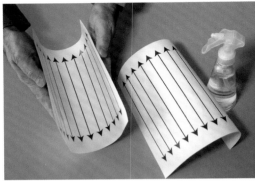

With the grain

If we could nominate one origami model that would be essential for every origami practitioner to master, it would be the traditional Japanese Crane. When folded well, it embodies the best of origami's promise: engineering elegance and a graceful style. We have developed a folding method and lesson that will improve your ability to fold wonderful examples of this classic design. The lessons hone key folding skills: determining the direc-

tion of the grain of the sheet of paper; installing the crease pattern; folding against the grain; accommodating for the paper's thickness and layers; skillfully executing inside-reverse folds; and forming precise, beautiful points. Mastering these skills will improve all of your subsequent folding.

We recommend and often use this particular model as a tool, not only to evaluate the skill level of an incoming student, but also to evaluate and learn

from different types of papers. Akira Yoshizawa, considered by many to be the father of expressive origami art, once said, "Before you start, you must know the nature of paper." Paper is not just one material but a huge family of infinitely diverse products. For this exercise, explore folding the traditional Japanese Crane several times from same size squares, but each time, fold paper with different properties. After that, explore folding larger and smaller squares of only one material. Folders refer to "relative thickness" to describe the key relationship between the size of the square and its thickness. You will be able to fold an acceptable crane from a smaller square if it is thinner. Soon, you should be able to evaluate the thickness of any paper, and instinctively know what size square will work best.

Properties: Each particular type of paper is engineered and manufactured with a purpose in mind. Specified ingredients are processed in the manner that results in the desired properties for that need. In this lesson, you will become familiar with three of the most important physical properties of the papers readily available to origami enthusiasts: grain, rigidity, and thickness.

Let's first explore grain. Grain is produced in the papermaking process, which starts by beating plant fiber to a pulp while adding water. The hydrated pulp fibers become randomly oriented when suspended in a vat of water. These fibers can be removed from the

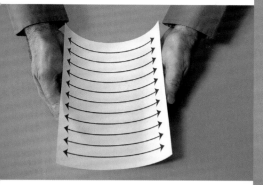

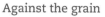
Against the grain

Left: Three sheets of paper, soft, medium, stiff.

Below: Different materials and sizes will affect the paper's folding properties.

vat and dried into any shape (pulp casting), but when the pulp is removed from the slurry using a flat screen, the process is called "sheet forming." The direction of the motion of the screen raising the watery pulp out of the slurry tank produces the grain because it aligns a majority of the fibers along the direction of the water flow. Grain noticeably impacts the structure of paper when it is dried. Highly grained papers typically fold more easily in the direction of the grain, while resisting any folds attempted across the grain. Similar looking materials often fold quite differently because of their grain, and so the origami student should experiment by folding a familiar model from squares of different materials cut to the same size, in order to evaluate the effects of the grain.

Now consider rigidity or stiffness. Paper may be soft and cloth-like, or as

stiff as a board (with the majority being somewhere in-between). Plant species, age, harvesting, and beating (pulp preparation) may all impact the stiffness of the paper. Various substances commonly added, such as natural glues, synthetic polymers, mineral fillers, and applied coatings may also affect the paper's stiffness.

Finally, consider the paper's relative thickness, which expresses the thick-

ness measurement and the size of the sheet as a ratio. A typical 6 inch (15 cm) square sheet of solid color origami paper is about 2/1,000 of an inch (or 0.05 mm) in thickness. A sheet of paper that is four times as thick would also need to be four times the length to have the same relative thickness. Conversely, a sheet of half the length would have to be half the original thickness to have the same relative thickness. Every origami project will have an optimum range of relative thickness, an important consideration when scaling the size of the model up or down.

An Origami Rule of Thumb: Many folders instinctively sharpen the creases of their origami with a fingernail or thumbnail. However, the sharp edge of your thumbnail could bruise, mar or even rip the paper! You can avoid this if you turn your nail slightly over to apply pressure with a smooth portion of the back (top) of the nail. Use a suitable tool (such as the bowl of a spoon or a "bone folder") instead of your thumbnail if you are folding for many hours, or working with rough or heavy paper. Traditionally, so-called "bone folders" were carved of bone, but most are now hardwood, metal, stone or molded plastic. Whatever you choose, make sure the folding tool will not scar or discolor the paper.

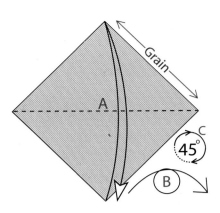

1 Begin with the paper right side up, diamond-wise, and with the grain running parallel to the top right edge. (A) Valley-fold diagonally in half. Unfold. (B) Turn over, left to right. (C) Rotate 45 degrees clockwise.

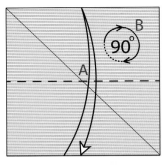

2 Notice that the diagonal crease should run from the top left to the bottom right corners, and that the grain is horizontal. (A) Valley-fold in half, bottom to top. Unfold. Here, you have just folded along the direction of the grain. Perhaps you noticed that the paper offered very little resistance to your effort. (B) Rotate 90 degrees clockwise.

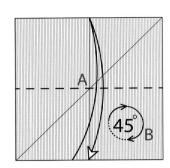

3 Notice that the diagonal crease now runs from the top right to the bottom left corners and that the grain is vertical. (A) Valley-fold in half, bottom to top. Unfold. (B) Rotate 45 degrees clockwise.

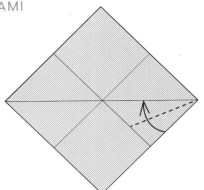

4 If you have correctly followed the folding sequence and orientation of the paper up to this point, then the "wrong" side of your paper will display two perpendicularly intersecting valley creases and one horizontal diagonal mountain crease. The grain of your paper should be running parallel to the bottom right edge. If so, then you are properly set to make your first corner-narrowing crease, and you will be folding with the grain, which is easiest. Valley-fold the upper half of the bottom right edge to align with the horizontal mountain crease. Stop the fold when it intersects the 45-degree angled valley crease.

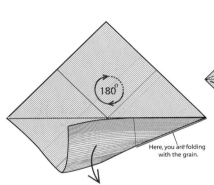

Here, you are folding with the grain.

5 Did you feel how easy it was to control the fold cleanly to the corner of the square? You were folding with the grain. Unfold the paper and rotate 180 degrees.

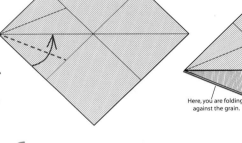

6 Valley-fold the upper half of the bottom left edge to align with the horizontal mountain crease. Stop the fold when it intersects the 45-degree angled valley crease.

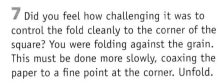

Here, you are folding against the grain.

7 Did you feel how challenging it was to control the fold cleanly to the corner of the square? You were folding against the grain. This must be done more slowly, coaxing the paper to a fine point at the corner. Unfold.

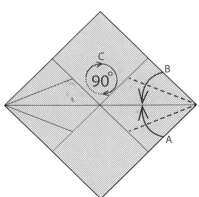

8 (A & B) Repeat steps 4 through 7 at the opposite corner. (C) Rotate 90 degrees.

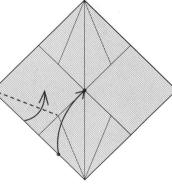

9 It is best to first fold with the grain; so, we must begin at the lower half of the left corner, where the grain runs in our favor. Valley-fold the bottom left edge upward, making it perpendicular to the vertical center crease. Use the point where the intersection of creases marks the center to ensure that the angle of your fold is correct.

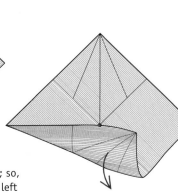

10 Unfold.

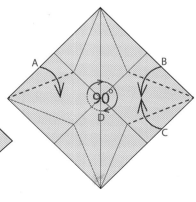

11 (A, B & C) Install the remaining three corner-narrowing creases. (D) Rotate the paper so that the diagonal crease is horizontal.

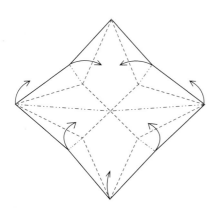

12 Use the existing valley (blue) and mountain (red) creases to collapse the form. Look ahead to figure 13 for the shape.

13 Rotate the paper 180 degrees.

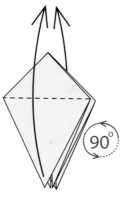

14 One at time, valley-fold the front and the back flaps up, as far as they will go. Rotate the paper 90 degrees counterclockwise.

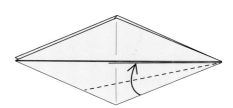

15 Notice that the horizontal split is on the right. Valley-fold the bottom right edge very close to the center split. This space should taper to nothing by the time the fold reaches the right end corner. It is best to leave a small space between the folded edge and the split, to facilitate a clean reverse fold at step 19.

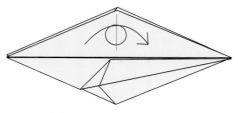

16 Turn over, left to right.

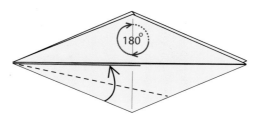

17 Repeat step 15, then rotate the paper 180 degrees.

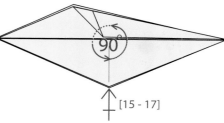

[15 - 17]

18 Repeat steps 15 through 17, then rotate the paper 90 degrees.

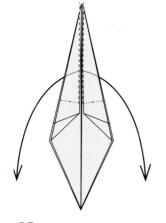

19 Inside-reverse-fold the narrow points down as far as they will go, aligning the outermost edges of all of the layers.

20 Valley-fold the front and back flaps up as far as they will go, flat.

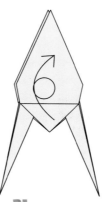

21 Turn over, top to bottom.

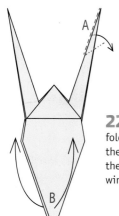

22 (A) Inside-reverse-fold the top of one of the vertical points for the head. (B) Bring the wings up, level.

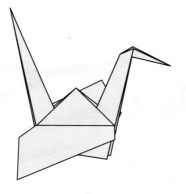

23 The Japanese Crane

Takeaways: Evaluation as Meditation

Paper folding can be a rejuvenating and meditative experience, especially when one has first mastered the folding sequence of the model. The hands will enjoy a fluid dance with the paper while the mind enjoys a spell of tranquility. Nevertheless, attaining mastery is often fraught with a series of stressful episodes and disappointments. Between these troubling episodes are opportunities to reset your calm by way of reflection and evaluation.

Hold the completed model in both hands, turning the piece calmly while studying every part from different points of view to vary the effect of lighting. Try to be critical but dispassionate, with a mind towards assessing a fair and rational evaluation of the results. Recall your folding experience of each point deserving of improvement. For the crane, you might spend as long as five minutes at the exercise. More should not be necessary. As with all meditations, breathe! Fold another crane.

Lessons from the Heart

designed by Michael G. LaFosse

LESSON: "DANCING WITH THE PAPER";
DRY FOLDING IN THE AIR

Folding against the surface of a table is much easier for beginners, and it is essential when first learning a model. However, many advanced origami techniques are best performed off the table while supporting the paper solely with your hands. Michael recalls his first meeting with origami master Akira Yoshizawa in 1991, at a master class held in Ossining, New York. Master Yoshizawa shared several nuggets of wisdom with this group of students, and some of it was "tough love" indeed. Michael recalled how the Master railed against folding paper against the table, "You do not dance with your back against a wall!" Lifting his paper, the master deftly folded the square diagonally in half. It was perfect. His hands performed the deceptively simple task with grace and confidence. Master Yoshizawa explained that he thought folding paper against the hard surface of the table eliminated the lyrical aspect of folding,

producing a lifeless product, and so, in order to create the most expressive origami art, one must fold the paper off the table and in the air.

People rarely use their hands with equal facility: a right-handed person usually places folds with that hand while securing the paper with the left, whether folding against a surface or in the air. The hand that you write with is also your dominant working, or "folding" hand; the other is your "holding" hand. And like partners in a dance, one leads as the other follows. At first, this can be challenging, and it may feel ugly and stilted. Michael likes to use his Lesson from the Heart as a practice *étude* to help his students work through the performance, developing the required support (for the strength and control) necessary for folding con-

fidently in the air. He calls this exercise "a conversation between two hands." Perfect it by rehearsing over and over again, so that you build a rhythm and cadence. Work to remove any awkward gaps interrupting the flow. With practice, folding in the air can become an enjoyable experience, and when you master this performance, it will also be quite lovely to watch.

Practice with the common papers that you have, such as 6-inch / 15-cm origami paper, or even the largest squares cut from letter-size printer stock. Begin your practice by folding the Lesson from the Heart against the surface of a table until you have learned the sequence by "Heart." Only when you are able to fold the model without referring to the instructions will you be able to put your full concentration on controlling these folds in the air. Use the same size and type of paper for each attempt until you have mastered it, and then challenge yourself with other paper kinds and sizes. We think you will be surprised at the level of control that you will develop, and we hope that you will adopt this little exercise as part of your origami performance repertoire.

Takeaways

I love what origami master Akira Yoshizawa once said, as quoted in Leland Stowe's article, Paper Magic of Origami, Beacon Magazine of Hawai'i, 1970: "For when we use our hands effectively, our hearts are most at peace." Another quote that I love is one spoken by origami artist, Paul Jackson, in the film Between the Folds, "The process of making is the point of it. The object looks good if the process felt good. This needs to be a kind of ballet." Indeed, Yoshizawa often spoke of folding masterfully as a kind of "dancing with the paper".

Master this model, and then "perform" it for, and give it to, a friend. You will know if you have presented a special moment by the watching the expression on their face, as they watch your graceful hands fashion this heart.

As a moment of meditation for yourself, try folding this heart to a favorite piece of music. Select a score that suits your folding style and one that will allow you plenty of time to savor every move!

This Origami Heart is dedicated to the memory of Mr. Yoshizawa.

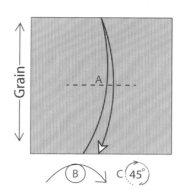

1 Begin right side up and with the grain running vertically.

(A) Valley-fold the center half of the square horizontally and unfold. Here, you are folding against the grain. This is a calculated effort to make steps 5 and 6 easier by folding with the grain. (B) Turn over, left to right. (C) Rotate 45 degrees clockwise.

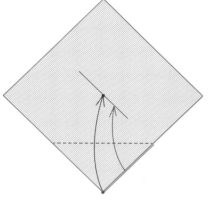

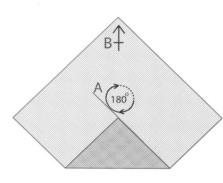

3 (A) Rotate the paper 180 degrees. (B) Repeat step 2, making the opposite corners meet at the center.

2 Notice that the grain is now running from the bottom left edge to the top right edge. Valley-fold the bottom corner to the center. Use the bottom half of the bottom right edge to align with the center crease. You will be folding against the grain.

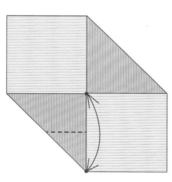

5 Valley-fold the bottom, obtuse corner to the center. Fold only from the left side limit to the center.

Unfold.

4 Rotate 45 degrees clockwise.

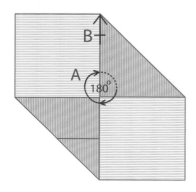

6 (A) Rotate the paper 180 degrees. (B) Repeat step 5.

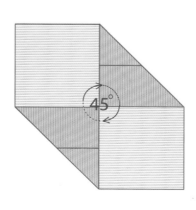

7 Rotate 45 degrees clockwise.

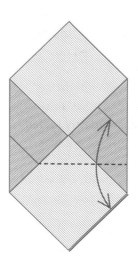

8 Valley-fold the bottom corner up, aligning the bottom right edge to the indicated crease. Fold only from the right side limit to the bottom end of the left side crease. Unfold.

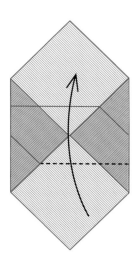

9 (A) Rotate 180 degrees. (B) Repeat step 8.

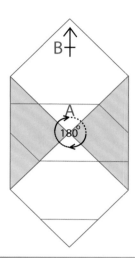

10 Your crease pattern should look like this. Use the bottom horizontal crease to move the bottom flap up.

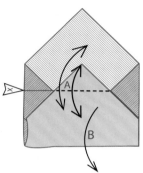

11 (A) Horizontally valley-fold the top corner of the front flap at the level of the horizontal crease of the back flap. Unfold. (B) Return the front flap to the bottom.

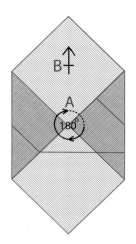

12 (A) Rotate the paper 180 degrees. (B) Repeat step 11.

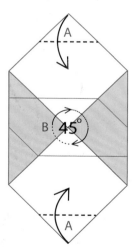

13 (A) Valley-fold the top and bottom corners inward. (B) Rotate 45 degrees clockwise.

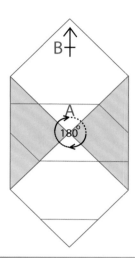

14 Your paper should look like this. Use the existing creases in sequence, closing the envelope. Creases at "D" will form upon flattening the model completely. Refer to the following photo sequence.

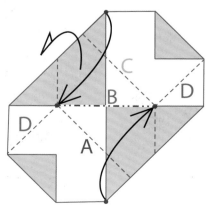

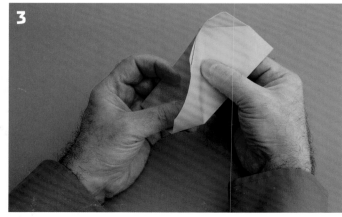

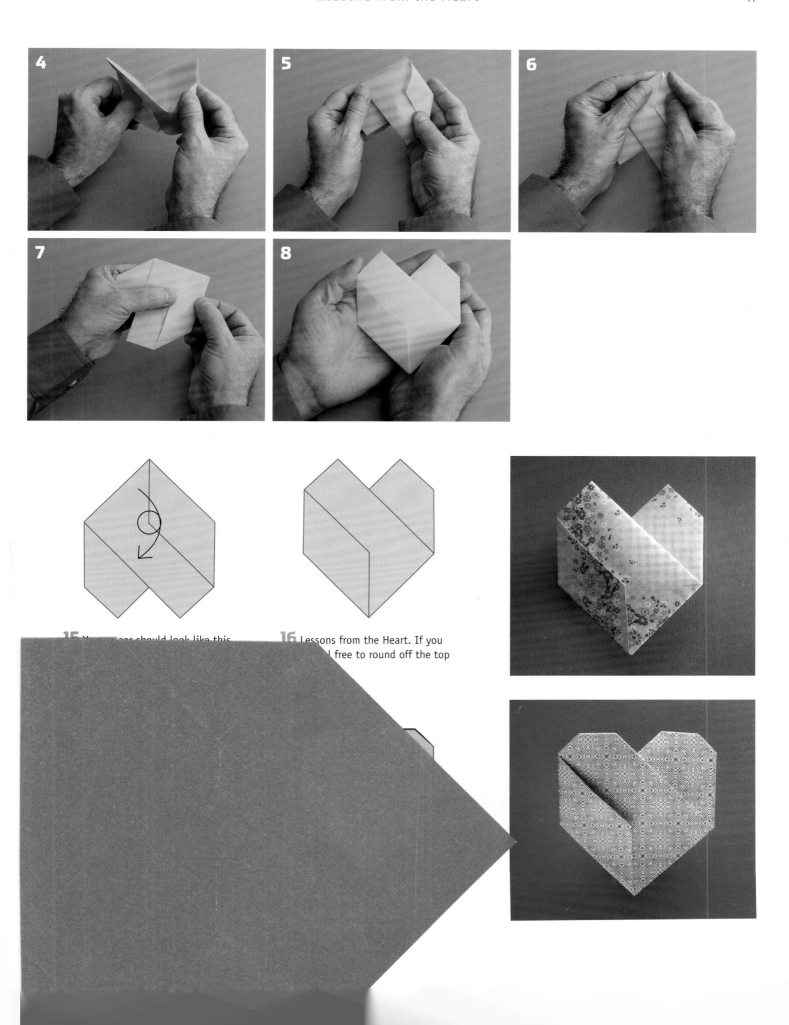

15 Your paper should look like this.

16 Lessons from the Heart. If you
feel free to round off the top

Anne LaVin's Squirrel

designed by Anne LaVin

LESSON: DESIGNING MINIMALIST ORIGAMI

Introduction by Anne LaVin

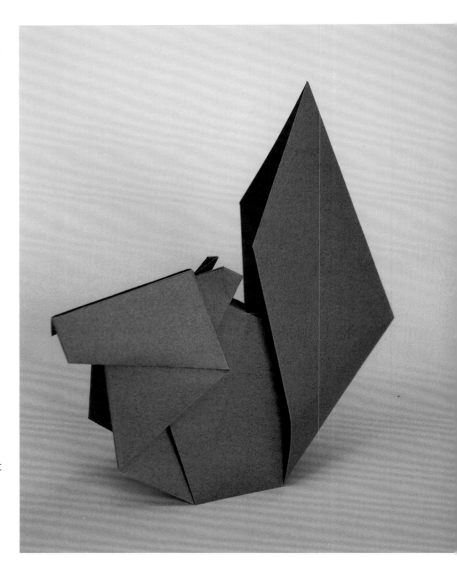

For me, designing this origami Squirrel was a lesson in abstraction. I created it in response to a challenge posed by members of an online group focusing on simple origami. Not only did we have the basic limitation of origami folded from one square with no cuts, but the folding sequence also had to be simple and short.

I knew I wasn't going to be able to represent everything about a squirrel, and so I decided to focus only on the visual elements that defined "squirrelness" best for me. During the long winters in northern New England, I get to know a lot of the local squirrel population — they are usually sitting at our bird feeders with their heavy winter coats fully fluffed out, flicking their wonderfully expressive tails — and so I decided to first focus on the tail. The visual volume of a squirrel's tail is huge (although mostly just hair and air). This meant that a lot of the paper would become the tail, and for efficiency, should probably contain as few layers as possible.

If one corner of the paper was to become the tail, the diagonal of the square could become the central axis of the creature, and so I folded the square in half diagonally. The tail should be a blunt point, and so I folded the corners in towards the middle, but without bringing the fold all the way to the corner. Aha! Perhaps a sort of mutant fish base would create a narrow point at the other end to allow me to shape the head, and the extra flaps could be ears. (I find the shape of a squirrel's ear especially cute, and so that would be another fun detail to refine.) After that, I fiddled with the proportions until it resembled a seated, fluffy squirrel.

I carefully marked the creases and intersections of the version that I liked most, unfolded it, and then I explored identifying the landmarks that would result in the correct proportions during a repeatable folding sequence. A few weeks later, with Michael's help, I was able to nail down the landmarks for the ideal proportions so Michael could diagram it.

— Anne LaVin

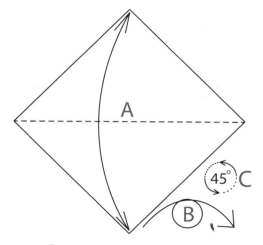

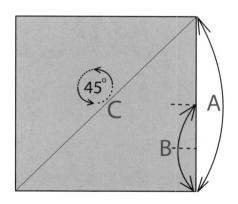

1 Begin with the white side up. (A) Valley-fold diagonally in half. Unfold. (B) Turn over, left to right. (C) Rotate 45 degrees counterclockwise.

2 Notice the orientation of the diagonal crease. (A) Valley-fold a short pinch mark at the midpoint of the right edge. Unfold. (B) Valley-fold a short pinch mark halfway between the first pinch mark and the bottom right corner. Unfold. (C) Rotate 45 degrees counterclockwise.

Takeaways: Do Not Overthink!

All origami is abstract, so embrace it as such! How few folds can be made to a square, yet still produce a recognizable squirrel? How few to produce one with a charming character? Which elements or specific folds contribute to that character? The flick of the tail? Cock of the ear? Tilt of the head? How did your choice of paper affect the "look," success or the viewers' perception of your creature? Distill.

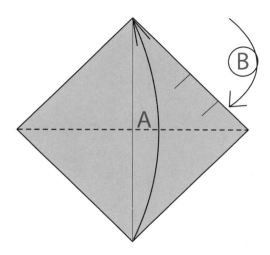

3 (A) Valley-fold diagonally in half, bottom corner to top. (B) Turn over, top to bottom.

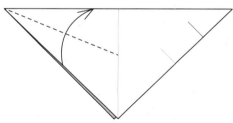

4 Check your paper to be sure that the two pinch marks are visible on the right side of the top layer. Valley-fold the left edge of the top layer to align with the top folded edge. Stop the fold at the vertical center crease.

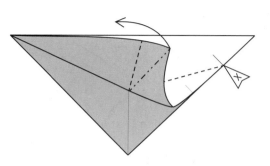

5 Mountain-fold the square corner in half and move it to the left. Valley-fold from the vertical center crease to the end of the topmost pinch mark and flatten the paper. This is an eccentric rabbit ear.

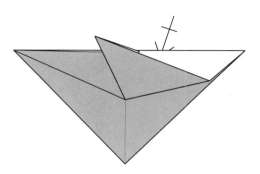

6 Your paper should look like this. Repeat on the other side. These flaps will become the ears.

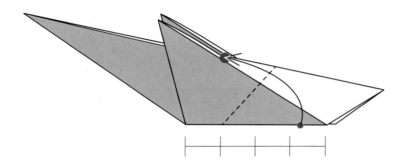

7 Valley-fold the right side of the paper over the left. Set the proper angle by pivoting at approximately one quarter the length of the bottom edge, beginning from the left end, and making one point of the bottom edge intersect with the "V" notch, above.

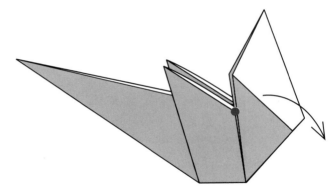

8 Your paper should look like this. Move the right side flap back down.

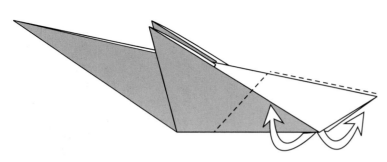

9 Turn the right side of the paper inside out, using the creases formed in the pervious step to guide the final shape. This will be the tail.

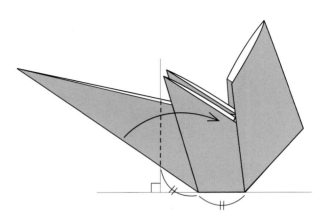

10 Use the length of bottom horizontal edge to estimate the starting point of this fold. Valley-fold the left side pointed flap to the right. The fold should be perpendicular to the horizontal bottom edge.

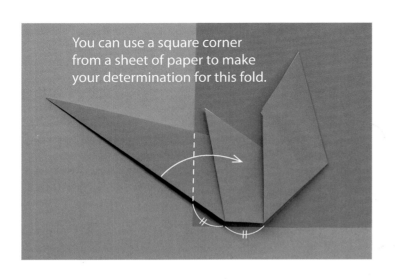

You can use a square corner from a sheet of paper to make your determination for this fold.

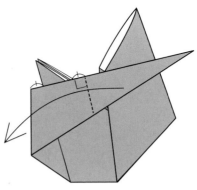

11 Use the length of top edge, from the front of the ear to the left corner, to estimate the starting point of this fold. Valley-fold the pointed flap to the left. The fold should be perpendicular to the line of the top edge.

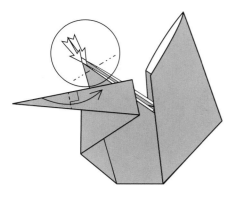

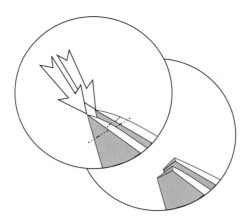

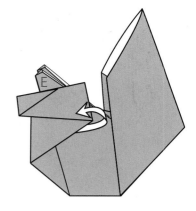

12 Valley-fold the pointed flap to the right, allowing a short forward length for the muzzle. The fold should be perpendicular to the line of the top edge. Inside-reverse-fold the tips of the ears.

13 Detail for folding in the ear tips.

14 Move ear layer "E" to the front.

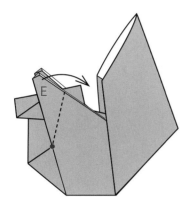

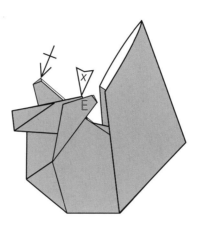

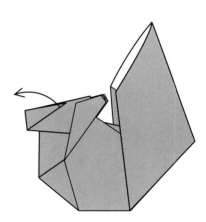

15 Valley-fold the front layer ear flap backwards. Use the intersection, marked in the diagram by a red dot, of two folded edges for the bottom end of the fold line.

16 Notice that the top edge of the ear lies below the top edge of the head, indicated by the "X" arrow. Fold the other ear to match.

17 Unfold the head flap.

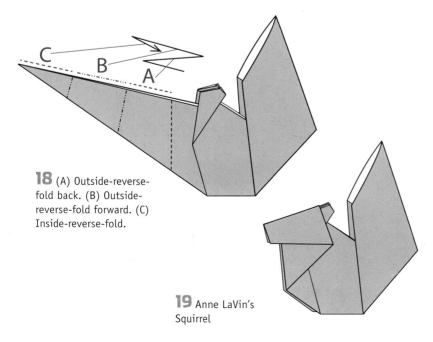

18 (A) Outside-reverse-fold back. (B) Outside-reverse-fold forward. (C) Inside-reverse-fold.

19 Anne LaVin's Squirrel

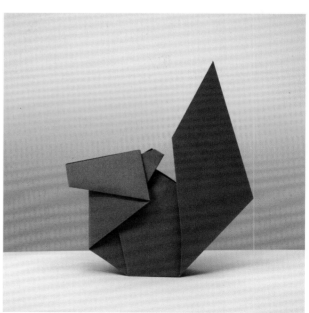

The Great White $hark

designed by Michael G. LaFosse

LESSON: WET-FOLDING PAPER MONEY

Here's a dollar bill model that requires wet folding. Great white shark sightings have been in the news regularly, both in Massachusetts, and in Hawai'i, and anyone with a toe in the ocean may be thinking about the probability of being mistaken for food. Humans are awed by the power, strength and violent feeding behavior of hungry great whites, but this doesn't excuse unwarranted fear of, or brutality to them. These magnificent creatures cruise the waters for hundreds of miles, surviving by culling the sick and the weak, and in so doing, making our sea life populations even healthier.

The quality of the paper used for US currency is superb because it is designed and formulated for strength and durability. It folds best when moistened slightly, as do other papers of similar quality fibers and blends. Moistening the paper before or while it is being folded is commonly called "wet folding." This leads to misunderstanding because the paper is not soaking wet — only slightly damp. Wet-folding offers several advantages to the origami artist: Once dry, the project will retain its physical form indefinitely (until it is moistened again); wet folding makes thicker and stiffer papers easier to fold; wet folding preserves the integrity of the fibers. (Dry folding, on the other hand, breaks some of the fibers and that damage weakens the paper. Wet folding allows the fibers to gently bend instead of breaking.) When wet folding, add just the least amount of moisture that will make the paper soft and yielding (more easily foldable). The paper should neither look wet, nor feel wet, but it will feel cool to the touch. New, crisp bills are the first choice for money origami projects, but you may partially restore a bill's foldability with a warm clothes iron. When selecting dollar bills for origami art, it is good to be fussy. Since individual bills are trimmed from large sheets with a high-speed cutting machine, the margins are often uneven, and so bills with perfectly symmetrical margins are hard to find. If you are folding a model that requires printing symmetry, select a bill with equal margins on the short ends. Some origami designs show both back and front (reverse and obverse) sides of the bill, and some designs look best when the two designs are registered. Alignment of the engraving plate's die strikes from front to back is easy to check by holding the bill up to the light.

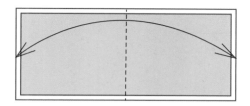

1 Valley-fold in half, short edge to short edge. Unfold.

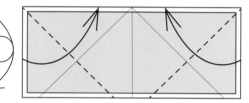

2 Valley-fold each of the bottom edge halves up to align with the center crease.

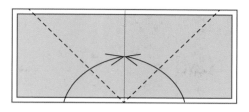

3 Your paper should look like this. Unfold.

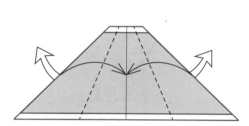

4 Turn over, top to bottom.

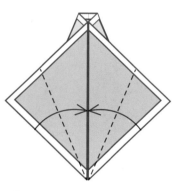

5 Valley-fold the left and right short edges to align with the top edge.

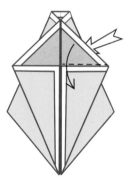

6 Turn over, top to bottom.

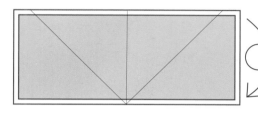

7 Valley-fold the left and right folded edges to align with the center crease. Allow the hidden triangular flaps to come from the back and lay on top.

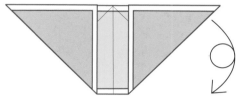

8 Valley-fold the bottom left and right edges to align with the vertical center split.

9 Open a pocket at the outside, top right — indicated by the white arrow — while valley-folding along the base of the associated triangular-shaped layer.

10 Open a pocket inside of the top right layer while continuing to valley-fold the associated triangular layer downward.

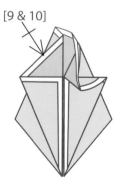

[9 & 10]

11 Repeat steps 9 and 10 to form an open hood shape at the top of the model.

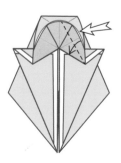

12 Valley-fold to collapse the right side of the hood shape to the center.

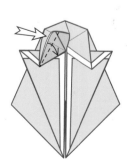

13 Repeat step 12 on the left.

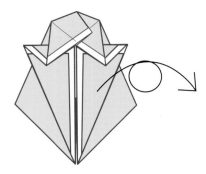

14 Turn over.

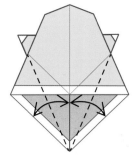

15 Valley-fold the bottom left and right edges to align with the vertical center. Unfold.

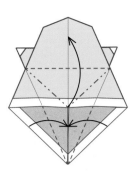

16 Use the creases to perform a petal-fold of the horizontal raw edge. Look ahead at the next diagram for the shape.

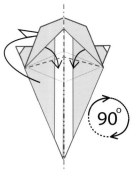

17 Rabbit-ear the triangular flap and mountain-fold the model in half lengthwise. Rotate 90 degrees clockwise.

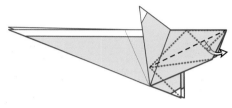

18 Pull out the hidden flap ("X") to make ready the paper for the mouth. Valley-folds will form inside as your complete this step. Firmly flatten the model at the front to secure the hidden valley folds. Look ahead at the next diagram for the result.

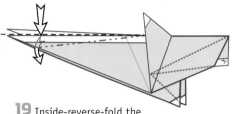

19 Inside-reverse-fold the topmost triangular flap at the back end of the model.

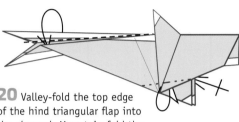

20 Valley-fold the top edge of the hind triangular flap into the channel. Mountain-fold the lower corners inside.

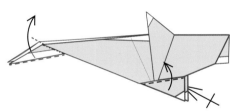

21 Reverse-fold the tail flaps together. Valley-fold the fin flaps upwards.

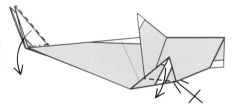

22 Valley-fold the leftmost flap down. Valley-fold the fin flaps down.

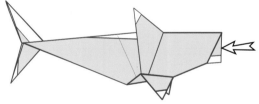

23 Form the mouth by opening out the sides slightly and pushing in at the center.

24 The Great White $hark

Takeaways: Wet Fold Your Paper Money!

Wet your paper money, it can take it! Have you ever forgotten a bill or two in your pocket, only to find that they have gone through the washing machine?

They emerge usable (and clean). Not a problem. In fact, your paper money will enjoy a little sip of water before your begin to fold, and will become supple and more relaxed. You too will be more relaxed as you fold, as you find the currency more compliant, especially when adding details with small folds. And when layers build up, the added moisture helps you compress them with only modest pressure. The dried bill will hold the new form that you so carefully crafted while it was moist.

I must say that we have encountered a good deal of resistance to the adoption of wet folding from among beginner to intermediate paper folders. Perhaps there is a perception of inconvenience; perhaps it is the difference in the folding experience that lacks appeal. We hope to change this attitude. The pros far outweigh the cons.

The Elegant — Simple Hummingbird

designed by Michael G. LaFosse

LESSON: DESIGN SIMPLICITY WHEN FOLDING FOILS AND PLASTICIZED PAPERS

Takeaways:
Take it Step by Step

One of the most useful tools that our students enjoy is making scrapbooks of their favorite models. We have a huge supply of tiny origami paper: 1½", 1¾", and 2" squares (often sold to be folded into individual flower petals). Each time a student progresses to the next step, they begin again with a new piece of tiny paper. At the end, they have a sequence of "step folds" that are easy to paste in a decorative arrangement into a scrapbook. When the model produces a three-dimensional object, they simply insert a snapshot in place of the 3-D object. What a great memory jog! This is as useful for seniors and older beginners as it is for our youngest folders. Try it!

This gem resulted from one of the many large commercial commissions that fell through. A major corporate client asked us to quote folding thousands of hummingbirds, but they wanted us to replicate or approximate another artist's design without their permission, and so we refused. We also felt that their proposed design was needlessly time-consuming and inelegant. Michael set out to design a different approach to the subject in a way that better captured the spirit of this wonderful creature, while also reducing the folding time. When we proposed his design solution, the job had already been farmed out to a folding factory. You can't win them all, and their loss is your gain! We know you'll love to fold this cutie to grace your cheerful greeting cards, table place cards and scrapbook entries. We think it perfectly embodies origami elegance and simplicity — the characteristic hallmarks of the time-honored and best-loved traditional models.

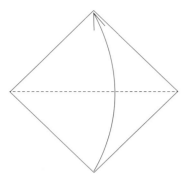

1 Begin with the "wrong" side up if using paper colored or textured differently on each side. Valley-fold in half diagonally, bottom corner to top.

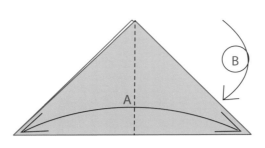

2 (A) Valley-fold in half and unfold.
(B) Turn over, top to bottom.

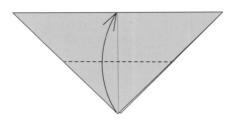

3 Valley-fold the bottom square corners to the middle of the top edge.

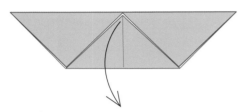

4 Unfold the triangular top layer flap.

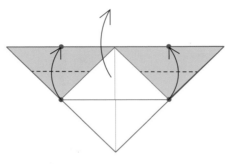

5 Move the triangular flap of the topmost layer up and beyond the top edge. Align the short horizontal crease from the base of the triangular flap with the long, horizontal folded edge. Valley-fold to flatten. Look ahead to see the shape.

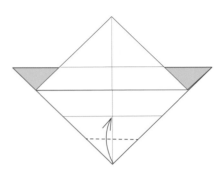

6 Valley-fold the bottom corner to the lowest intersection of creases.

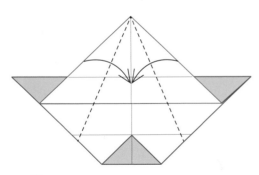

7 Valley-fold the top left and right edges to align with the vertical center creases.

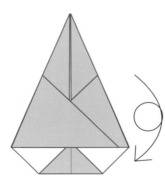

8 Turn over, top to bottom.

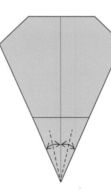

9 Valley-fold and unfold the bottom left and right edges to the center crease, installing two short creases in the bottom corner.

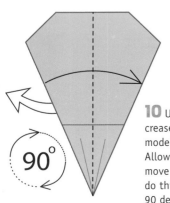

10 Use the vertical center crease to valley-fold the model in half, left to right. Allow the attached wing to move to the front as you do this. Rotate the paper 90 degrees clockwise.

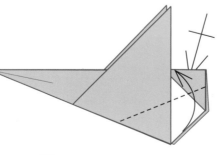

11 Valley-fold the bottom right edge to align with the horizontal top edge. Repeat behind.

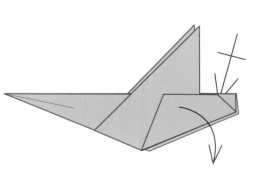

12 Unfold the front and back flaps.

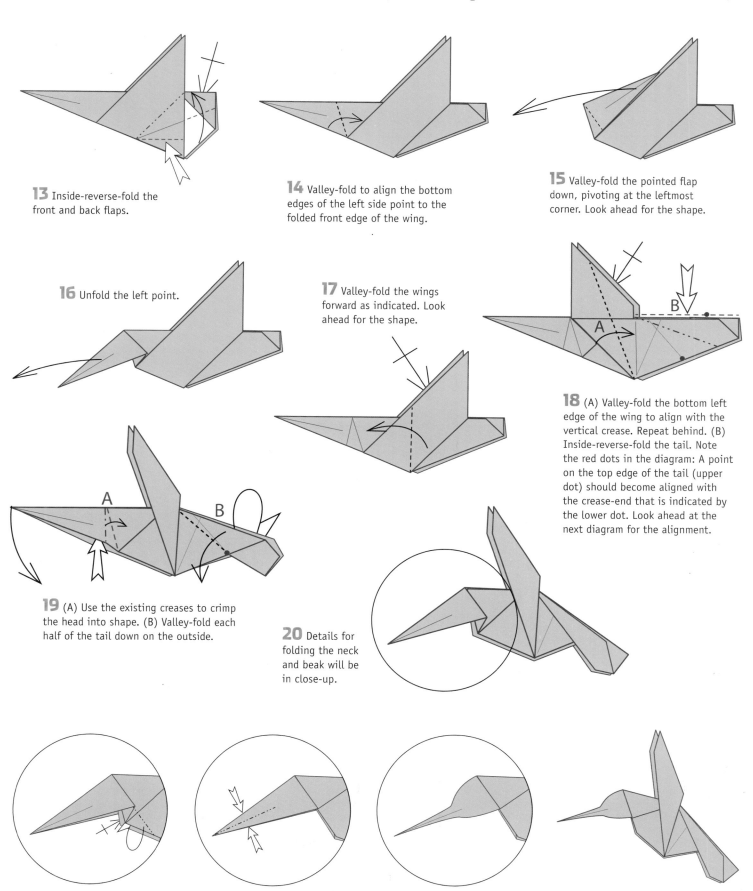

13 Inside-reverse-fold the front and back flaps.

14 Valley-fold to align the bottom edges of the left side point to the folded front edge of the wing.

15 Valley-fold the pointed flap down, pivoting at the leftmost corner. Look ahead for the shape.

16 Unfold the left point.

17 Valley-fold the wings forward as indicated. Look ahead for the shape.

18 (A) Valley-fold the bottom left edge of the wing to align with the vertical crease. Repeat behind. (B) Inside-reverse-fold the tail. Note the red dots in the diagram: A point on the top edge of the tail (upper dot) should become aligned with the crease-end that is indicated by the lower dot. Look ahead at the next diagram for the alignment.

19 (A) Use the existing creases to crimp the head into shape. (B) Valley-fold each half of the tail down on the outside.

20 Details for folding the neck and beak will be in close-up.

21 Mountain-fold the neck paper in.

22 Flatten the beak.

23 Beak complete.

24 The Elegant — Simple Hummingbird

The Dim Sum Bun

designed by Michael G. LaFosse

LESSON: A POEM FOR THE FINGERS

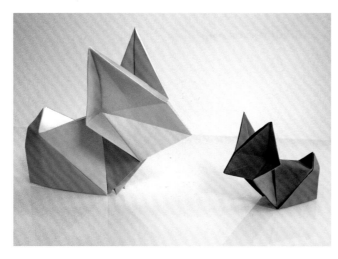

This little origami bunny makes your origami juices flow the way you salivate when the Dim Sum cart, fresh from the kitchen, approaches your table at a Chinese restaurant. This plump and tasty morsel represents a style of origami that Michael calls little "Poems for the Fingers." These are origami models we enjoy folding again and again, and because they are short and sweet, we love to share them with others. Just as a poem is a distilled and much shorter form of prose, this simple and quick composition displays a high level of abstraction. The geometric 3-D aspect, combined with a choice of cute poses, allows them to be displayed in interesting ways, particularly when folded in a rainbow of colors and sizes or arranged in active groups.

Takeaways: Making Legends

Michael and I once rescued a pair of baby bunnies and released them after they were strong and healthy. Years later, "Nibbles" and "Walnut" were frequent visitors to our front yard at night, and if we returned home after dark, we would often catch them in our head-lights while they were grazing on the lawn. Sometimes they would have company, such as Ambrose the Skunk, who appears in our next origami étude. Nibbles and Walnut have grown and probably hopped away, but their progeny abounds. We still have the fond memories of rescuing them, and then driving 20 miles to find canned cat milk and an eyedropper at a pet store, in order to raise them. Their romping and racing around the deck and into our flower pots, and their un-canny ability to strike and patiently hold a pose for a clumsy photog-rapher, inspired several delightful origami designs.

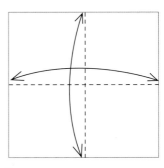

1 Begin with the "wrong" side up if using paper that is colored differently on each side. Valley-fold in half edge to edge both ways, unfolding after each.

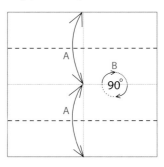

2 (A) Valley-fold the top and bottom edges to the horizontal center crease. Unfold. (B) Rotate 90 degrees.

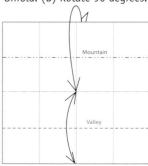

3 Valley-fold the bottom edge to the center. Unfold. Mountain-fold the top edge to the center. Unfold.

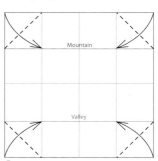

4 You now have a 16 square grid. Valley-fold each of the four corner squares in half diagonally. Notice the location of the horizontal mountain (top) and horizontal valley (bottom) creases. Preserve this orientation, relative to the folding in step 5.

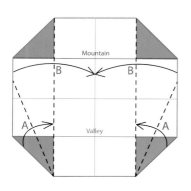

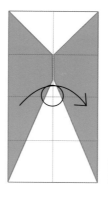

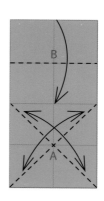

5 (A) Valley-fold the bottom left and right folded edges to the nearest vertical crease. (B) Use the existing vertical creases to Valley-fold the sides to the center.

6 Turn over, left to right.

7 (A) Valley-fold the bottom half diagonally both ways, unfolding after each. (B) Valley-fold the top edge down to the center.

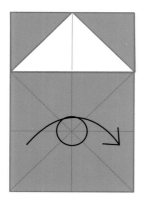

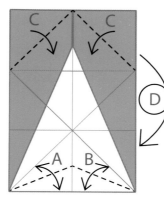

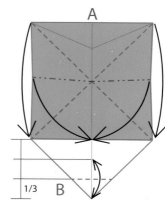

8 Turn over, left to right.

9 (A & B) Valley-fold each of the bottom two 45-degree angles in half, unfolding after each. (C) Valley-fold the two top corners down. (D) turn over, top to bottom.

10 (A) Use the existing mountain and valley creases to collapse the top, square area into a triangular shape. Look ahead at step 11 for the shape. (B) Valley-fold the bottom corner of the bottom triangular area one-third up. Unfold.

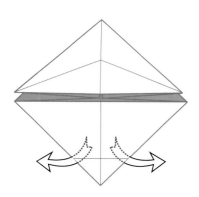

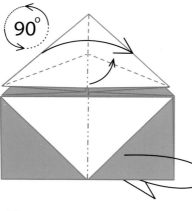

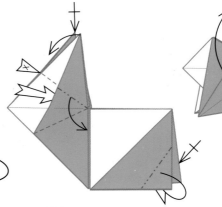

11 Move the bottom square corners out from the back.

12 Valley-fold the top triangular area in half to the right, while pushing the bottom edge of the triangle up. Use the existing creases to perform this maneuver. Mountain-fold the bottom layers in half, to the left. Rotate 90 degrees counterclockwise.

13 Your paper should look like this. Open the front of the ear. Valley-fold down at the bottom limits of the top layer. Squash-fold. Look ahead at step 14 for the shape. Repeat behind. Mountain-fold the bottom hind corners in.

14 Your paper should look like this. Pull the ears up.

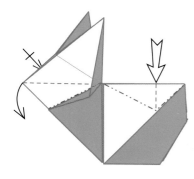

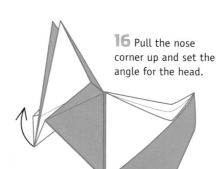

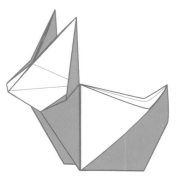

15 Move the end of the nose down and in between the layers of the front legs. Mountain and valley-fold the layers of the lower half of the head so that the paper is flat and well creased. Push down to flatten the back. Mountain-fold along the suggested lines to make a saddle-shape with the tail pointing up.

16 Pull the nose corner up and set the angle for the head.

17 The Dim Sum Bun

Ambrose the Skunk

designed by Michael G. LaFosse

LESSON: ORIGAMI INSIDE-OUT; MAKING "DUO PAPER" USING BACK COATING

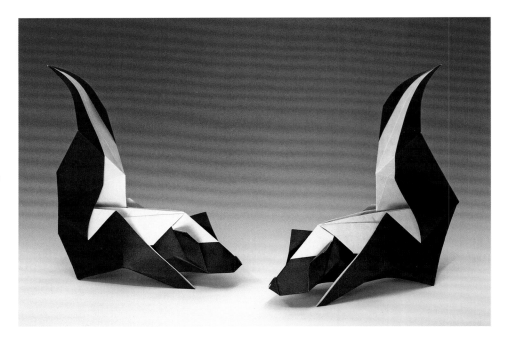

As you fold a piece of paper, you can create a series of enveloping layers, which gives you the potential to reveal some of the inside (reverse side of the paper) on the outside of the sculpture. Imagine this skunk folded from a single, solid color paper (without a contrasting white side on the reverse). It would be impossible to evoke the same reaction in the viewer, which affirms the power of designing so called "duo" models. Michael likes to think of two types of "Inside-Out" origami models. One is "Obligatory" or consequential color-change origami designs, that result in both sides of the paper showing, regardless of the intent — there is simply no way to produce that particular form without showing both sides of the paper.

He calls the other type, "Opportunistic" or creative choice color-change models, because they allow the designer to take advantage of showing some of the reverse side (or not), at his or her discretion.

This skunk is a good example of the latter. It allowed Michael to "play" with the amount and shape of the white paper that finally shows, by changing the landmarks to balance the effect. This provided the opportunity for him to reveal just enough white to make the creature immediately identifiable and endearing.

When looking for an opportunity to display the reverse side of the paper, look for raw edges. In those places, at least a portion of the reverse side can be folded over to the outside.

While this skunk can be successfully folded from commercial origami paper, this design presents a wealth of possibilities for expressive, artistic exploration, and you may want to create your own origami "duo" papers by using methylcellulose paste to back coat a fine piece of light-toned paper onto a fine piece of darker paper. Let these skunks, folded of fancy-patterned papers, liven up your next party table.

Takeaways:
Two Sides of the Same Coin

If you consider color-change designs as fun puzzles to solve, make a list of bi-colored subjects, and then give designing them a try. Don't restrict your list to white-bellied critters; even popular symbols, shapes, and alphabet letters appearing on a white background are fair game. Chances are good that other origami designers have taken a whack at designing something to fill the bill, but don't let that stop you. There is more than one way to skin a skunk. When you begin to design for color change opportunities, try folding familiar designs from larger sheets of duo (two-color) paper that has first been blintzed (corners folded in to the center, either all on one side or a mixture of front or back). Another handy trick is to form a square from a 2:1 rectangle by folding the end quarters over (perhaps one quarter to the front and the opposite to the back). US paper currency is also great "duo" paper, with black printing on one side, and green on the other. When you find that you have developed a knack for bringing certain colors exactly where you want them, then do the same with images on the paper money. It is fun to design origami animals that take advantage of the little swirls as eyes, or the whorls as horns.

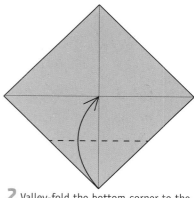

1 Valley-fold diagonally in half, both ways, unfolding after each. Turn over, left to right.

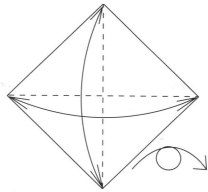

2 Valley-fold the bottom corner to the center where the creases intersect.

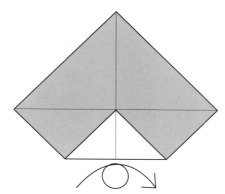

3 Turn over, left to right.

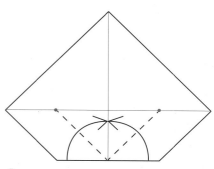

4 Valley-fold the left and right halves of the bottom edge to align with the vertical center crease. Stop each fold at the horizontal center crease.

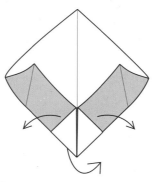

5 Unfold completely.

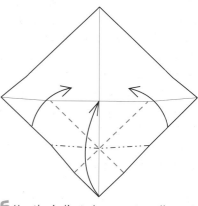

6 Use the indicated creases to collapse the bottom area, using both mountain- and valley-folds. Look ahead at the next drawing for the shape.

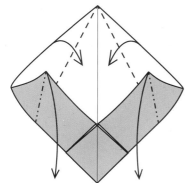

7 Mountain-fold the left and right corners in half and pivot downward. Valley-fold from each pivot point to the top corner.

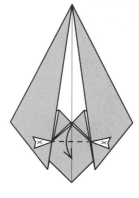

8 Your paper should look like this. Valley-fold the top center corner down, folding at the level where the corner's edges intersect with the inner edges of the left and right flaps.

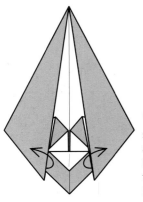

9 Swap layers so that the left and right flaps lay underneath the paper for the head.

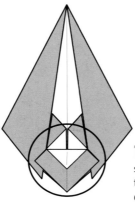

10 Your paper should look like this. Head folding details to follow.

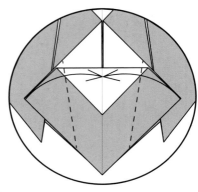

11 Valley-fold the left and right corners to meet high on the vertical center crease.

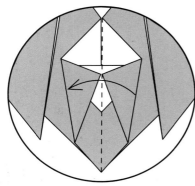

12 Valley-fold the right half of the head to the left.

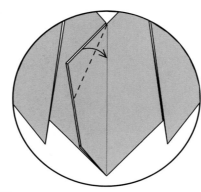

13 Valley-fold the top edge of the top layer to align with the vertical center crease.

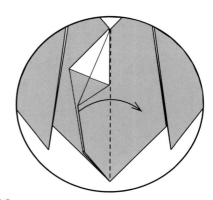

14 Valley-fold the top layer to the right.

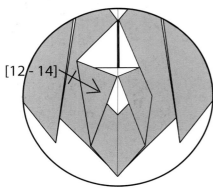

[12 - 14]

15 Repeat steps 12 through 14 on the left.

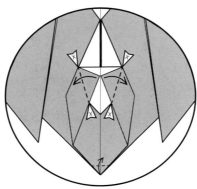

16 Valley-fold the indicated corners out, using the limits marked in the drawing to form the ears. Valley-fold the bottom corner up for the nose.

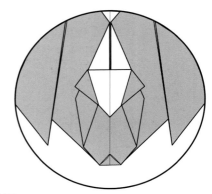

17 The completed head.

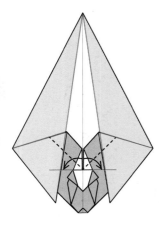

18 Valley-fold the partially hidden layers down so that the vertical edge of each layer lies horizontally at the level of the top of the head.

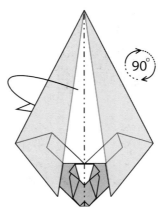

19 Mountain-fold in half lengthwise, and rotate 90 degrees clockwise.

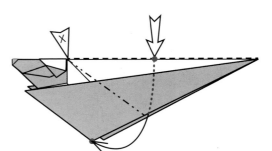

20 Inside-reverse-fold the tail, pivoting at the top of the head, marked by the "X" arrowhead, and stopping when the inside-reverse-folded edge intersects the corner of the hind foot.

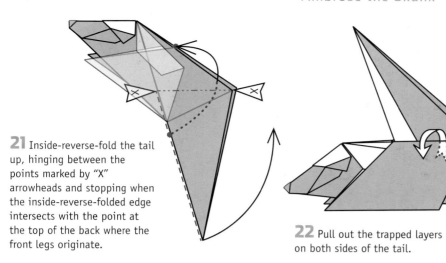

21 Inside-reverse-fold the tail up, hinging between the points marked by "X" arrowheads and stopping when the inside-reverse-folded edge intersects with the point at the top of the back where the front legs originate.

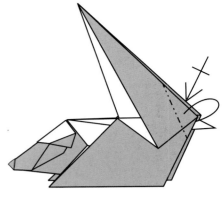

22 Pull out the trapped layers on both sides of the tail.

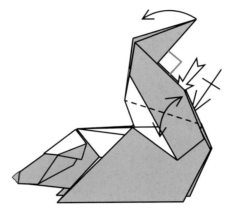

23 Mountain-fold the back corners inside the tail.

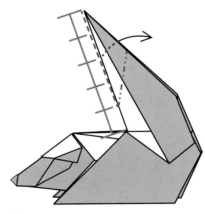

24 Inside-reverse-fold the top four-fifths of the tail. Look ahead to see the 90-degree reference mark in red, in the next step.

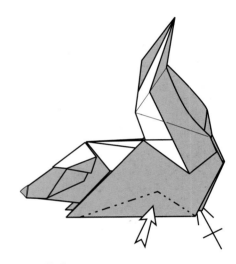

25 Valley-fold a hinging crease on both sides of the tail, spanning from the base of the inside-reverse down to the base of the tail, at the level of the back. Open the top of the tail.

26 Make angled sets of mountain folds and on the left and right sides of the body, defining the front and hind legs. Make these folds through all layers on each side.

27 Lift up the ears. Make angled sets of mountain folds on the left and right sides of the neck, up along the jaw line and down to connect with the crease end, indicated by the red dot. (A cutaway view of the outermost layer of leg paper reveals the hidden layer.) Curl the tip of the tail.

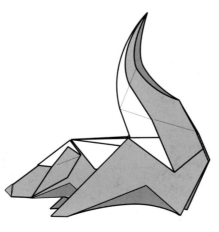

28 Ambrose the Skunk

A Seahorse for Al Miyatake

designed by Michael G. LaFosse

LESSON: DEVELOPING FINE MOTOR CONTROL

Seahorses are remarkable creatures that have nothing in common with horses except for the shape of their heads. Even those head features make them look like caricatures or cartoon versions, carved in cuteness. Nobody every got bucked by a briny bronco, nor stampeded by a saltwater stallion. We hope every reader has a chance to watch the behavior of real live seahorses. The males "give birth" to the young, and there is no shortage of variety in size, appearance or favorite habitat. If we discover anything like these creatures on another planet, we would no doubt write books and make movies about them. We depend upon our oceans for food, recreation, transportation and even climate moderation, but the oceans' health requires healthy nursery reefs and coastal wetlands. Millions of tropical fish fanciers decorate their homes with saltwater

tanks populated with colorful and fascinating fish. When they purchase wild creatures, it puts immense pressure on the natural populations of seahorses. Al Miyatake is a long-time

friend and supporter living on the Kona coast of the Big Island of Hawai'i. Al pointed out that aquaculture has come to the rescue, and they now have a seahorse farm to supply the aquarist's demand for "reef ponies"!

This étude exposes you to a folding algorithm, the sequential crimping pattern to produce a spiral tail. Origami spirals are fun to fold, and they produce beautiful, interesting angles and shadows. We participated in an exhibit called "Spiritual Geometry," where artists contributed works that explored "magical" relationships of shapes and proportions that have fascinated artists and mathematicians for centuries. Origami can be a useful tool for understanding some of these relationships, such as the Pythagorean theorem, and various spiral folding algorithms, such as the one used to shape this Seahorse's tail.

Takeaways: The Power of Art to Change Behavior

We are often invited to discuss the possibilities of incorporating origami into an educational program about the Earth's unique habitats and their iconic creatures. Being biologists by training, we are always eager to participate. Museums have hired us to design origami versions of creatures from New England, the Sonoran Desert, the polar extremes, East Coast flyways, the Florida Everglades and our fragile reefs and oceans. In every case, the hope is that by folding

origami versions of these subjects, youngsters will take a closer look at those creatures and their habitats, develop an understanding of the issues surrounding their very survival, and hopefully seek out more information about how they can make a positive difference for our future.

Even more engaging is when the origami is made by the visitor's own hands, because Origami renditions of subject species become tangible icons that visitors fold, hold and keep. Origami art has recently proven to be an engaging way to raise the level

of public awareness to the pending extinction of the polar bear, elephant, rhino and several endangered butterflies. Can you identify a creature or plant, struggling for existence, that might be helped if people were made just a little more aware about how their choices impact the lives of the other inhabitants that share this special speck in the universe? It need not be rocket science: we designed origami dogs to help raise awareness (and money) for a local no-kill animal shelter. Go local and start small. Have fun while helping a critter!

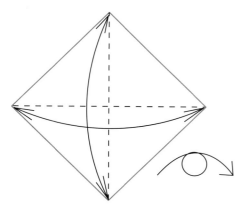

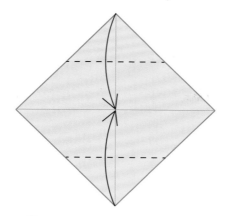

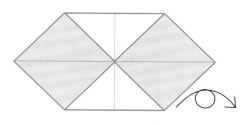

1 Begin "wrong" side up. Valley-fold in half diagonally both ways, unfolding after each. Turn over.

2 Valley-fold the top and bottom corners to meet at the middle.

3 Your paper should look like this. Turn over, left to right.

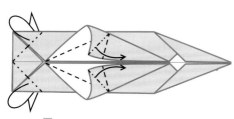

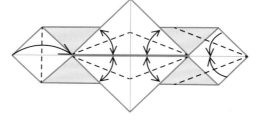

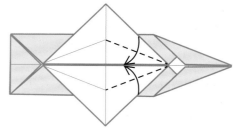

4 Valley-fold the top and bottom edges to meet at the middle, allowing the backside triangular flaps to come to the front.

5 Valley-fold the left corner in. Valley-fold and unfold each of the four edges of the center square to the horizontal center. Valley-fold the top and bottom right edges to meet at the horizontal center.

6 Bring the top and bottom right edges of the center square to the horizontal center.

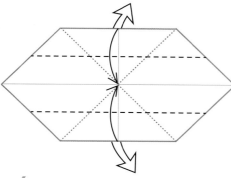

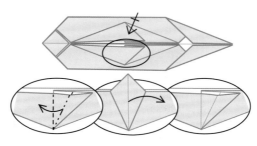

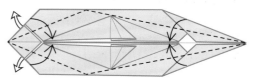

7 Mountain-fold the top and bottom square corners in half while folding them flat and to the right. Mountain-fold the left-side square corners behind.

8 Detail: Squash-fold the indicated corner into the shape of a kite. Unfold. Repeat with the corner above.

9 Valley-fold the top and bottom edges of the left side to meet at the center, allowing the triangular flaps at the back to come to the front. Valley-fold the left and right edges of the right corner to meet at the center.

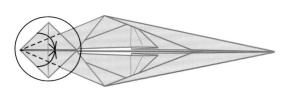

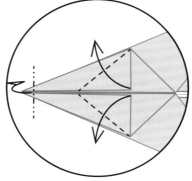

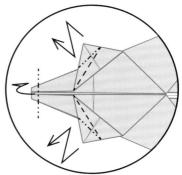

10 Head detail: Valley-fold the top and bottom left edges to meet at the center.

11 Mountain-fold the tip of the corner behind. Valley-fold the topmost square corners out.

12 Mountain-fold a small portion of the left end behind. Valley- and mountain-fold the indicated portion of the triangular flaps to form the head fins.

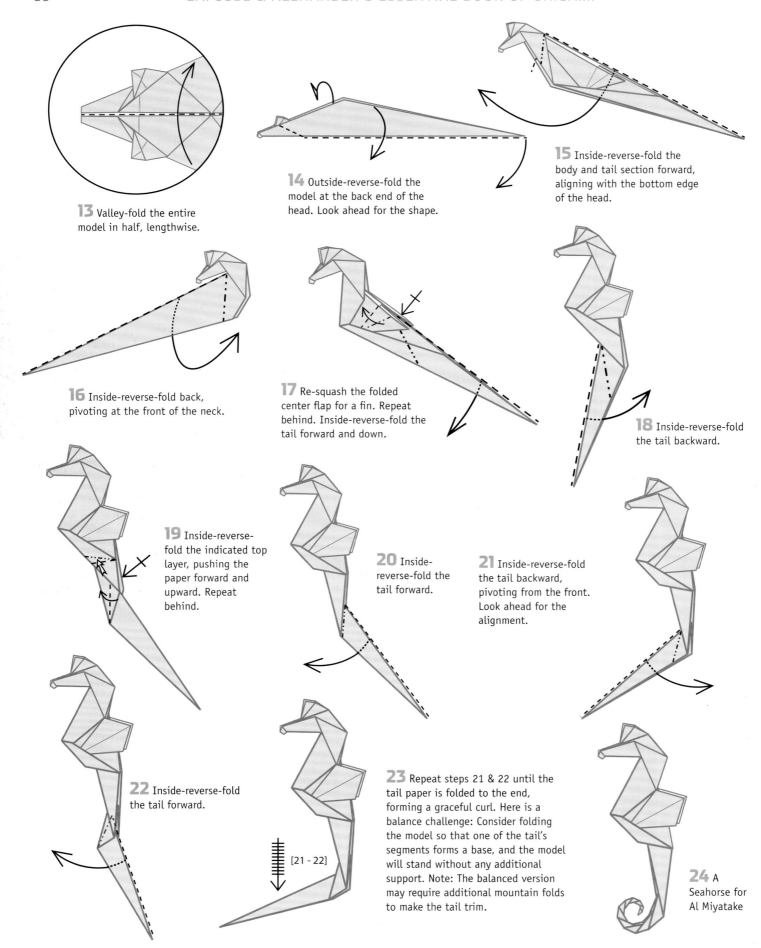

13 Valley-fold the entire model in half, lengthwise.

14 Outside-reverse-fold the model at the back end of the head. Look ahead for the shape.

15 Inside-reverse-fold the body and tail section forward, aligning with the bottom edge of the head.

16 Inside-reverse-fold back, pivoting at the front of the neck.

17 Re-squash the folded center flap for a fin. Repeat behind. Inside-reverse-fold the tail forward and down.

18 Inside-reverse-fold the tail backward.

19 Inside-reverse-fold the indicated top layer, pushing the paper forward and upward. Repeat behind.

20 Inside-reverse-fold the tail forward.

21 Inside-reverse-fold the tail backward, pivoting from the front. Look ahead for the alignment.

22 Inside-reverse-fold the tail forward.

[21 - 22]

23 Repeat steps 21 & 22 until the tail paper is folded to the end, forming a graceful curl. Here is a balance challenge: Consider folding the model so that one of the tail's segments forms a base, and the model will stand without any additional support. Note: The balanced version may require additional mountain folds to make the tail trim.

24 A Seahorse for Al Miyatake

Humuhumunukunukuapua'a

designed by Michael G. LaFosse

LESSON: **OBSERVING AND TRANSLATING KEY PROPORTIONS**

Often diagrams will illustrate a maneuver on one side only for efficiency, and then indicate (with just an arrow) to repeat the same on the other side. This often requires folding the mirror image of the maneuver. Some students struggle with this, and so this model will exercise spatial recognition and translation, in order to produce the mirror image. Why would you want to learn this? In this case, the fish is swimming to the right, but there may be reasons that you will want to frame another fish facing the other way. How about making origami jewelry — a pair of earrings for instance?

Tropical fish are the showy "butterflies" of the reef. Both are intricately beautiful, and when folded of brilliant pearlescent papers, will evoke the complexity and flamboyance of what these creatures choose to "wear." Upon closer inspection, there are usually

only two or three colors, but with a high contrast, accentuating the simple layout to their "graphic" designs.

From an origami design point of view, the distinctive angles of this fish's body, forehead and stripes provide a challenge to our ability to mimic what we observe. The eyes also seem to be set in a peculiar position. To us, the fish seems to "lean back" and defer to the more aggressive-looking creatures. Sometimes the "body language" of a body plan accurately describes the creature's character, as with the gentle, rounded, slowly-swimming manatee.

What makes this peculiar fish so compelling? For one thing, if you swim too close, it grunts like a pig! Also known as the "reef triggerfish," the Humuhumu (for short) has a piggy snout and bright red on its undersized pectoral fins. The Humuhumu is a highly territorial and solitary feeder, often

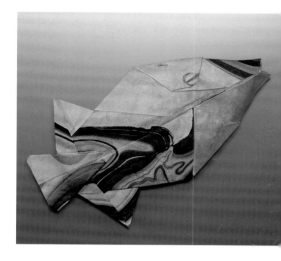

seen darting here and there, sucking up and squirting out sand from its distinctive, blue lips. When threatened, it can change colors or wedge itself tightly into crevices. Those distinctive lines form a bright yellow-outlined directional arrow on Humuhumu's back. If you happen to be fancy, its best to have other survival tricks up your sleeve!

Takeaways: Observing Patterns in Nature

What child hasn't pondered the distinctive stripes of a zebra? From the youngest age, we humans are fascinated by patterns. Friedrich Froebel, the German inventor of Kindergarten, spent much of his childhood in the vast woods near his home, and was captivated by the patterns he saw in nature: seed pods, floral whorls, tree branching and even the angles of rock crystals. He worked hard all of his life to understand the underlying causes of patterns. As a crystallographer, Froebel understood that the structure of atoms

and their numbers of electrons dictates how they can pack together, combine with other atoms, or as with water, form a lighter expanse of solid crystals when frozen.

Biology uses patterns too, the most common generated by cell growth around parent cells. Fibonacci described the pattern that creates spirals when the last two cells create another by doubling their sum. Charles Darwin was responsible for developing thoughts about how individuals with slight differences were sometimes favored when conditions changed, and how this natural selection nudged

along the success of species displaying the variety of patterns and forms that we see on Earth today. Biology exploits shape, whether it is the sticky, spikey surface of a virus particle, or the light-hungry reach of a giant oak tree's leafy branches. We also recognize pattern similarities between biological and non-biological entities, such as the whorl of microscopic mollusks and of spiral galaxies. It seems fitting that we are entertained by forming pleasing patterns simply by folding paper: we approximate the patterns that matter makes of itself — both invisibly small and incomprehensibly grand.

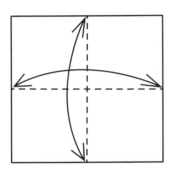

1 Begin with the "wrong" side up. Valley-fold in half edge to edge both ways, unfolding after each.

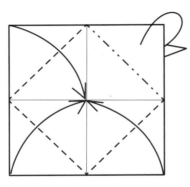

2 Valley-fold three corners to meet at the center on the front side. Mountain-fold the remaining corner to the center on the back side.

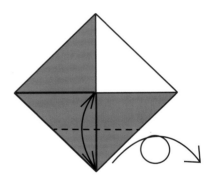

3 Be sure that your paper is oriented as shown in this drawing. Valley-fold the bottom corner to the center. Unfold. Turn over, left to right.

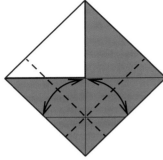

4 Again, be sure that your paper is oriented as shown. Valley-fold the bottom left and right edges to the center, unfolding after each.

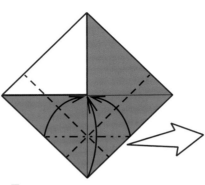

5 Use the mountain and valley creases to collapse the paper. Look ahead at the next drawing for the shape.

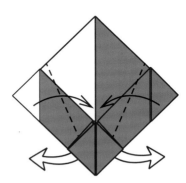

6 Valley-fold the left and right edges to meet at the vertical center. Allow the triangular flaps to come from the back and display behind the topmost square.

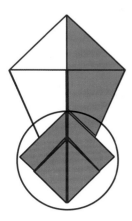

7 Folding details to follow. This area will form the tail fin, and the dorsal and ventral fins located at the back.

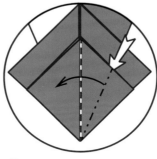

8 Squash-fold the right side of the topmost square area.

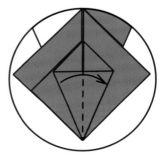

9 Valley-fold the left flap to the right.

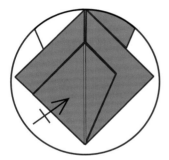

10 Repeat steps 8 and 9 on the left.

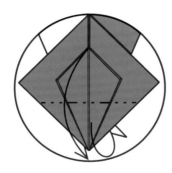

11 Your paper should look like this. Mountain-fold the bottom corner to the back. You will notice that as you proceed with the fold, a natural, centering limit will form as the inside layers emerge and form pockets. Look ahead to the next drawing for the shape.

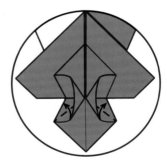

12 Valley-fold the bottom edges of the left and right pockets upward and squash-fold the pockets.

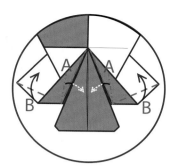

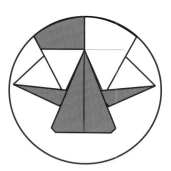

13 Valley-fold the bottom corner to touch the intersection of the folded edges above.

14 Notice that the folded edge at the bottom of the tail fin does not meet with the left and right corners. This effect makes the lobes of the tail fin look slightly rounded. Turn the model over, left to right.

15 Valley and mountain-fold to trim the fins, tucking center-aligning flaps under the top layers of the tail paper. Move the edges labeled "A," first, then those labeled "B." Look ahead at the next drawing for the shape.

16 Your paper should look like this.

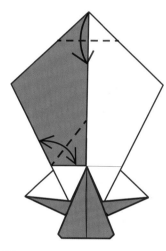

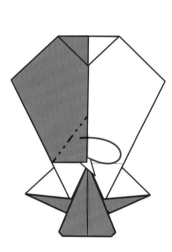

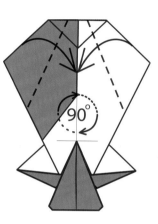

17 Valley-fold the top corner down. There is no landmark for this. Copy the proportions approximately. Valley-fold the short edge of the square corner of the top left layer to align with the outer left edge. Unfold.

18 Mountain-fold the square-cornered flap under the top layer.

19 Valley-fold the top left and right edges to meet at the vertical center. Rotate the paper 90 degrees clockwise.

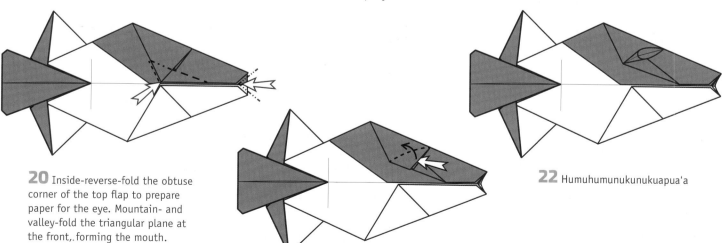

20 Inside-reverse-fold the obtuse corner of the top flap to prepare paper for the eye. Mountain- and valley-fold the triangular plane at the front, forming the mouth.

21 Open the top layer of the eye paper and squash-fold slightly to round it out.

22 Humuhumunukunukuapua'a

Yellow Tang for Mariko

designed by Michael G. LaFosse

LESSON: PREPARING PAPERS WITH PEARLESCENT AND LUSTER PAINTS

The west coast of the Big Island of Hawai'i was once called the "Gold Coast," not because of any precious metals lying about, but because of the bountiful schools of yellow tang, little fish so numerous that they made the surf zone appear yellow. The scales of the tang are tiny, and photogra- phy doesn't do their true beauty justice. For this model, we use paper doped with pearlescent luster pigment to mimic the sheen produced by the animal's miniature scales.

Now that you have tried wet fold- ing, we hope you appreciate its many benefits. There is another handy meth- od that our students enjoy that avoids some of the problems of fully wetting the papers — especially machine made papers with pronounced, often trou- blesome grain. We call it "Zone Fold- ing," and it involves applying moisture only where you need it, and only when you need it. We often use a folded nap- kin or paper towel, but even a moist- ened cotton swab works well because there is less likelihood of adding too much water. This design for the Yel-

Back coating to laminate a sheet of luster paper

Once you have rehearsed this model sufficiently, prepare a special piece of back coated yellow luster paper for your display piece: Lightly moisten a sheet of thin, white washi, and then brush a coat of yellow luster pigmented paint (from the craft store) onto one side. Allow it to dry fully. Moisten it once again, but this time, brush the reverse with methylcellulose gel and fold it in half. Re- strain the folded sheet while it is allowed to dry by pasting four edges to a rigid surface. Trim to the desired square size and wet fold the Yellow Tang for Mariko.

low Tang for Mariko is a bit unusual because it was planned for only one side to show, as if it were displayed on a Christmas tree. It works well when mounted in a shadow box frame, or on a pin-back to be worn as a brooch. Challenge your brain by folding other-handed examples from the same set of diagrams!

First, learn this model by practicing with letter printer paper. (Trim one end to make the largest square.) It might also help to practice this model with a piece of gold or yellow foil. After you are satisfied with your knowledge of the folding sequence, wet fold another from a piece of yellow tant or similar paper.

Takeaways:
Paper Can Be Like a Skin

Origami subjects depicting creatures from the river, pond, lake or the sea look wet when folded from paper made with just a hint of mica. Butterflies, birds and other natural history creatures folded from papers made with these luster pigments also seem to love the gallery lights. Acrylic-based luster paints available in craft stores are formulated for airbrush applications, but they also work just fine when applied to pre-moistened papers with a conventional paintbrush. Try several brands and colors to see which of these produce your favorite luster-enhanced papers.

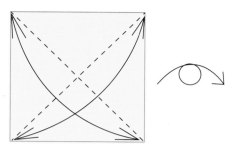
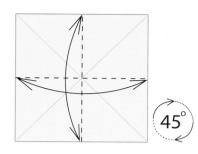

1 Valley-fold diagonally in half both ways, unfolding after each. Turn over, left to right.

2 Valley-fold in half edge to edge both ways, unfolding after each. Rotate 45 degrees.

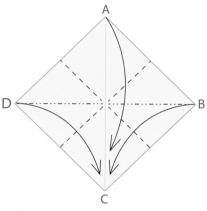
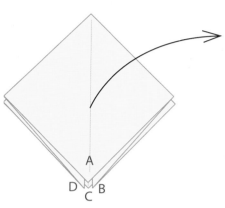

3 Use the mountain and valley creases to collapse the paper with all four corners meeting at the bottom.

4 Pull the top layer up and move it to the right, diagonally folding layer "A" in half.

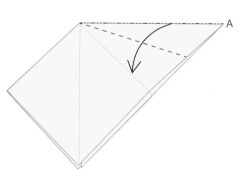
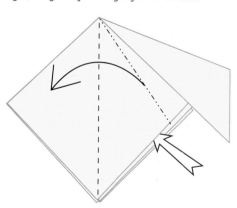

5 Valley-fold the top edge to align with the crease below.

6 Squash-fold. Look ahead for the alignment.

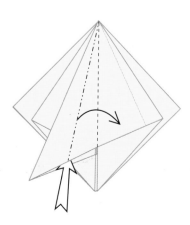

7 Squash-fold the topmost triangular flap.

8 Mountain-fold the square corner of the top layer inside.

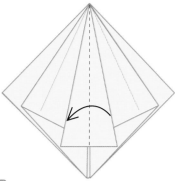

9 Valley-fold the top layer in half, right to the left.

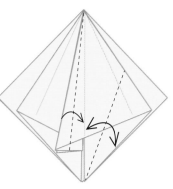

10 Valley-fold the top left edge to align with the vertical center. Valley-fold the outer top edge to the vertical center. Unfold.

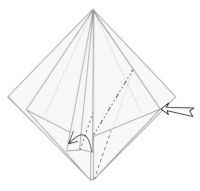

11 Valley-fold the bottom corner of the top left flap to the left, forming one lobe of the tail fin. Inside-reverse-fold the top layers on the right.

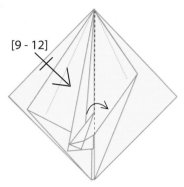

[9 - 12]

12 Valley-fold the center flap over. Repeat steps 9 through 12 on the left.

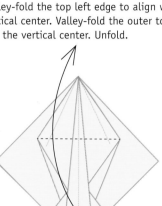

13 Valley-fold the tail flap up.

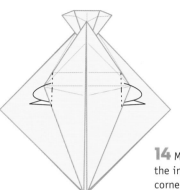

14 Mountain-fold the indicated corners behind.

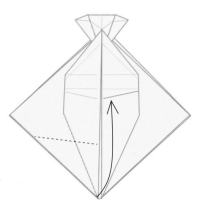

15 Valley-fold the bottom left flap up, making it touch the highlighted crease. Look ahead to step 16 for the angle.

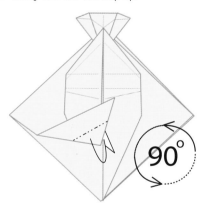

16 Mountain-fold the bottom corner of the triangular flap behind. Rotate 90 degrees counterclockwise.

90°

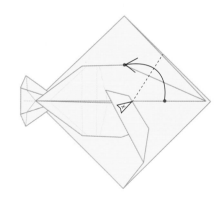

17 Valley-fold the top right flap to the left, making the bottom edge intersect the top front corner of the body, while guiding the bottom of the fold to the front edge of the pectoral fin, marked here with an "X" arrowhead.

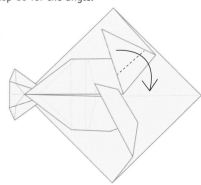

18 Valley-fold a portion of the triangular flap down and forward of the leading, folded edge. Look ahead for the proportion and angle.

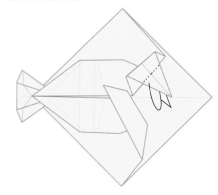

19 Mountain-fold the excess of the triangular flap behind.

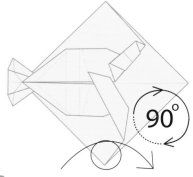

90°

20 Rotate 90 degrees clockwise, and turn over, left to right.

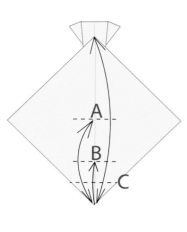

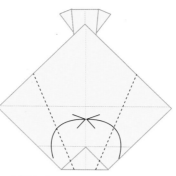

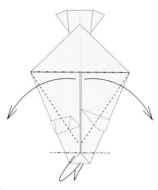

21 (A) Mark the center by valley-folding the bottom corner to the top, making a short pinch mark. Unfold. (B) Valley-fold a new pinch mark halfway between the first pinch mark and the bottom corner. Unfold. (C) Valley-fold the bottom corner to the bottom pinch mark.

22 Valley-fold the bottom left and right edges to meet at the vertical center.

23 Mountain-fold the bottom behind, folding at the level where the vertical folded edges diverge. Valley-fold the square-cornered flaps out.

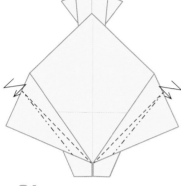

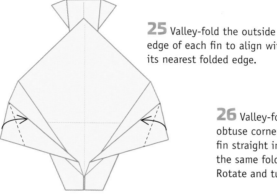

25 Valley-fold the outside edge of each fin to align with its nearest folded edge.

26 Valley-fold the obtuse corner of each fin straight in to touch the same folded edge. Rotate and turn over.

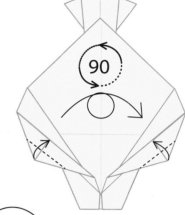

24 Valley- and mountain-fold the left and right flaps, forming detail pleats in the fins.

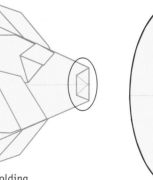

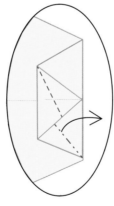

28 Slide the top layer of the bottom half of the mouth forward and squash-fold.

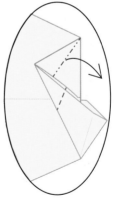

29 Slide the top layer of top half of the mouth forward and squash-fold.

27 Details for folding the mouth to follow.

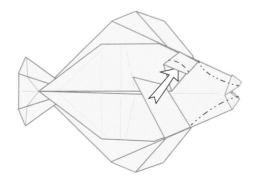

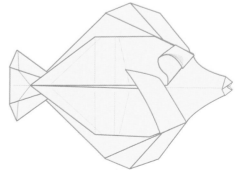

30 Your paper should look like this.

31 Open and round the eye. Make gracefully curved mountain-folds, narrowing the snout.

32 Yellow Tang for Mariko

Foley (or FOALie) the Pony

designed by Michael G. LaFosse

LESSON: SERENDIPITY AND HAVING FUN!

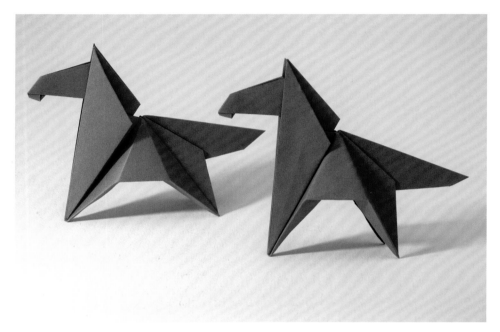

Purists may complain about this model with only three legs, because of course, a *real* horse has four. To paraphrase the thought expressed by origami professor Paul Jackson, from his interview in *Between the Folds*, Vanessa Gould's Peabody-Award-winning documentary film about origami, "Is an origami horse with four legs really better than one with only three?" That depends: If the four-legged version doesn't make a galloping sound, we'd rather fold a three-legged version that does! We fondly remember origami designs of the 1960s, when three-legged renditions of quadrupeds were common. There was something innocent and delightfully fanciful about those designs.

Foley (named after the great Hollywood sound-effects pioneer, Jack Foley) is a talented pony. Although he has only three legs, he can do something that few other origami ponies can do: make his own sound effects! This characteristic is achieved when you fold Foley from brightly-colored "origami papers." This paper is good fodder for folders because it is made from inexpensive wood pulp. Now found in large department and craft supply stores, it is the modern-day descendent of the first commercially packaged folding papers used in Kindergartens. It is ideal for designers: It is pre-cut perfectly square in handy sizes, and comes in a wide variety of colors and patterns. The majority of simple to intermediate origami designs work well when folded from this paper simply because the designer probably used it when designing the model.

Make the sound of the clacking hooves of a galloping horse by repeatedly moving the legs together and apart.

Takeways: Serendipity Folding

One satisfying feature of this model is the clicking sound that "Foley" makes as the legs are flexed back and forth. This effect will be produced only when Foley is folded from a crisp sheet of paper — not from softer papers, such as fine handmade long-fiber washi. I would love to be able to tell you that it was forethought and great intelligence that led me to design origami that produces a sound like a horse trot, but it was a simple case of serendipity.

When designing new origami, I take into consideration many factors: will this model be for an exhibit, or just for fun?; is it intended for the beginner, intermediate or for the advanced student?; is it to be an abstraction or highly detailed?; is it to be published in a book, taught in a classroom or posted to the Internet? The weight of these factors dictates which papers to use in my folding investigations. In the case of Foley, I thought that it would be best to use any thin, crisp paper, widely available to the hobbyist. That's when it "clicked." The cheap, crisp paper spontaneously produced the wonderful sound effect when I moved the horse's legs into the final stance. Brown wrapping paper works great for larger models.

1 Use paper that is colored that same on both sides. Valley-fold in half diagonally both ways, unfolding after each. Turn over and rotate 45 degrees.

2 Valley-fold in half edge to edge both ways, unfolding after each. Rotate 45 degrees.

3 Use the existing creases to collapse the paper, making all four corners meet at position "A."

4 Valley-fold corners "C" and "A" down.

5 Valley-fold the indicated top flaps down.

6 (A) Fold the triangular flap to the back. (B) Bring the triangular flap up. (C) Valley-fold in half, corner to corner, and unfold.

7 Align the crease, indicated in red, with the top, horizontal edge. Valley-fold to flatten.

8 Pull the flap up.

9 Open the flap. Use the creases formed in step 7 to crimp the flap down. Look ahead for the shape.

10 Your paper should look like this. Valley-fold the indicated short edge to the horizontal crease. Repeat behind.

11 (A) Valley-fold along the left side folded edge. Then reverse this fold to the back, making it flexible. (B) Valley- and reverse-fold along the right side, folded edge, making it flexible. (C) Valley-fold a short crease that bisects the right half of the bottom square corner. Reverse this fold to make it flexible.

12 Unfold the indicated small triangular flaps, front and back. Pull the large triangular flap up to unfold it.

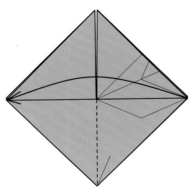

13 Move the top layers of the right half to the left, like turning the page of a book.

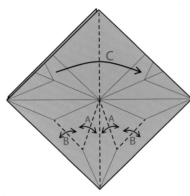

14 Your paper should display the symmetrical crease pattern shown here in blue. (A & B) Valley-fold and unfold to install these four connecting creases. (C) Valley-fold the top layer of the left side to the right.

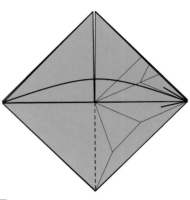

15 Move the top layers of the left half to the right, like turning the page of a book.

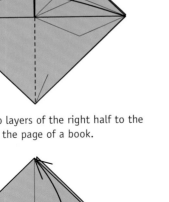

16 Valley-fold the top corner to the bottom. Return the corner to the top.

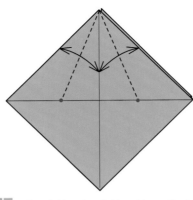

17 Valley-fold and unfold to bisect the left and right halves of the top square corner.

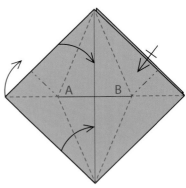

18 (A) Use the existing creases to form a Rabbit Ear, center corner pointing up. (B) Form a Rabbit Ear, center point up. Look ahead at step 19 for the shape.

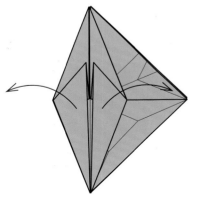

19 Unfold both Rabbit Ears.

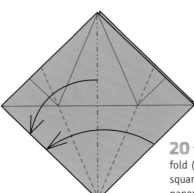

20 Valley-mountain-valley-fold (radial fan pleat) the square diamond, moving the paper to the left side to collapse the form. Look ahead for the shape.

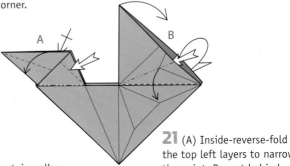

21 (A) Inside-reverse-fold the top left layers to narrow the point. Repeat behind. (B) Reinstall the crimp for the top right flap.

22 Your paper should look like this. (A) Crimp the left half of the paper. (B) Inside-reverse-fold the indicated flaps, front and back.

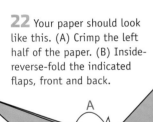

23 (A) Pull out. (B) Valley-fold the indicted flap up. Repeat behind.

24 (A) Inside-reverse-fold for the tail. (B) Mountain-fold a narrow portion of the horizontal left edge downward. Repeat behind.

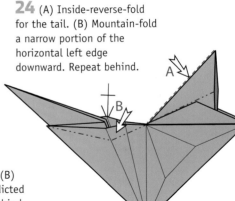

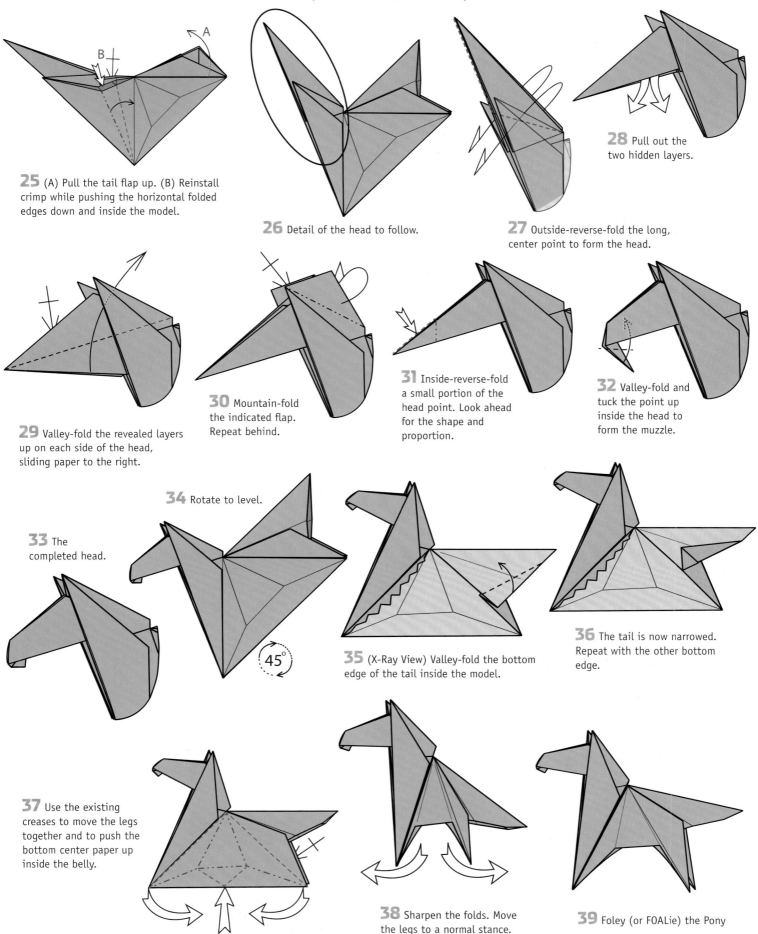

25 (A) Pull the tail flap up. (B) Reinstall crimp while pushing the horizontal folded edges down and inside the model.

26 Detail of the head to follow.

27 Outside-reverse-fold the long, center point to form the head.

28 Pull out the two hidden layers.

29 Valley-fold the revealed layers up on each side of the head, sliding paper to the right.

30 Mountain-fold the indicated flap. Repeat behind.

31 Inside-reverse-fold a small portion of the head point. Look ahead for the shape and proportion.

32 Valley-fold and tuck the point up inside the head to form the muzzle.

33 The completed head.

34 Rotate to level.

45°

35 (X-Ray View) Valley-fold the bottom edge of the tail inside the model.

36 The tail is now narrowed. Repeat with the other bottom edge.

37 Use the existing creases to move the legs together and to push the bottom center paper up inside the belly.

38 Sharpen the folds. Move the legs to a normal stance.

39 Foley (or FOALie) the Pony

The Happy Good-Luck Bat

designed by Michael G. LaFosse

LESSON: UNDERSTAND HOW THE PAPER'S GRAIN IMPACTS FOLD PLACEMENT DURING WET FOLDING

The commercial art paper that we recommend for this model is readily available in a wide variety of colors. It is inexpensive, and fun to fold, but it also has a pronounced grain. This is neither bad nor good, but do be mindful of it when you are wet folding any "grainy" type of paper. Grain is a characteristic of all machine-made papers, and of many handmade papers. If you think of fiber strands and their component cellulose fibrils as analogous to cooked spaghetti in a pot, and then imagine the paper making screen as the fork-like device that grabs at the spaghetti to pull it out of the water, it may be easier to understand how fibers will "line up" side by side on the screen as it is pulled out of the paper-making vat. This alignment or grain would not matter, but for the fact that the cellulose fiber's width increases more dramatically than the length whenever the moisture content increases. Imagine

how an emaciated cactus swells after a rainfall. Paper with grain is like a row of saguaro cactuses standing side-by-side. Add water, and none get taller, but they all get wider.

Because we wet fold our sculptural pieces, water is being evaporated throughout the folding process, causing the fiber widths to change, and so water must be added periodically. When this model is wet folded, it will make a big difference whether you place the folds by matching landmark points (as beginners often do), or by bisecting angles (which produces sharp points at the vertices). If the paper is cut when dry (as is recommended) try folding the first few steps after wetting, and you will soon see that the triangle has grown in one dimension more than in the other. This model will help you think differently about wet folding, making you less likely to use one side of the model as a placement template whenever you are using moistened, thicker, machine-made, highly grained papers. It will help you plan ahead in the future when locating points and handling flaps.

Takeaways: The Style's the Thing

It is possible that beginning paper folders rarely think much about the way that origami, as other art forms, has a variety of distinct styles. When you have explored a subject by approaching it in several different styles, you might be surprised what you learn when you compare how the results differ. An artist's choice of style greatly affects the spirit of each piece as perceived by the viewer.

Consider this simple bat folded in the style of the traditional, Japanese origami crane, displaying only flat planes and straight edges. Try folding one of these bats that way to compare the visual impact. Which do you prefer? For me, the geometrically planar version looks rather severe compared to the more lyrical, puffed-up, round-chested, jovial bat, which appears to delight in its flight!

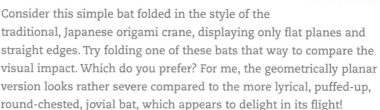

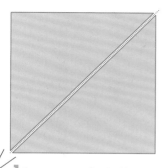

1 Cut a square of suitable paper diagonally in half. Each right-isosceles triangle makes one bat.
Using a moistened cloth or paper towel, swipe the back of a triangle.

Notice how the paper curls as moisture makes only the wet side swell.

Repeat the moistening step on the reverse side.

In a few moments, the paper will soften uniformly, and feel like a piece of cool leather.

2 Valley-fold the two bottom acute corners to the top right-angle corner.

Notice how the length of one flap is longer. That means that the grain runs perpendicular to the length of the flap! Don't worry. When the paper dries, all will be well. Unfold.

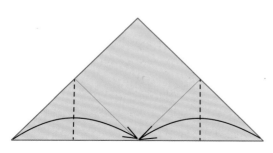

3 Valley-fold the two bottom acute corners to meet at the middle of the bottom edge.

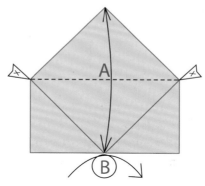

4 (A) Valley-fold the top corner down. Be sure that the fold spans between the two corners indicated by the "X" arrowheads. Unfold. (B) Turn over, left to right.

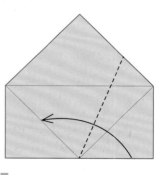

5 Valley-fold the right half of the bottom edge to align with the 45 degree-angled crease on the left.

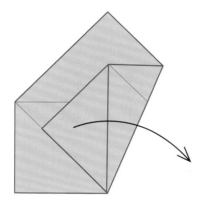

6 Your paper should look like this. Unfold.

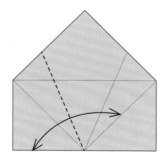

7 Valley-fold the left half of the bottom edge to align with the 45 degree-angled crease on the right. Unfold.

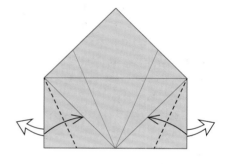

8 Valley-fold the left and right vertical edges to align with the 45 degree-angled creases. Allow the hidden triangular flaps to come to the front.

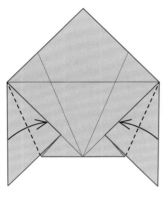

9 Valley-fold the left and right vertical edges to align with the 45 degree-angled folded edges.

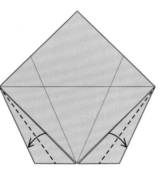

10 Valley-fold the topmost triangular flaps in half, longest edge to the second longest edge.

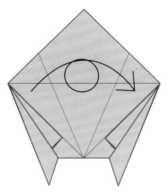

11 Turn over, left to right.

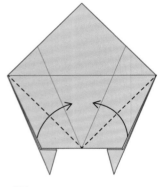

12 Use the 45 degree-angled creases to valley-fold the topmost flaps inward.

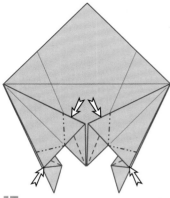

13 Your paper should look like this. Inside-reverse-fold each of the four double-layered corners.

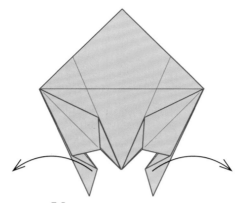

14 Your paper should look like this. Open the wings.

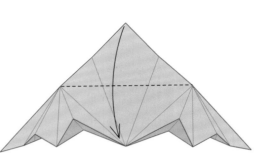

15 Use the existing crease to valley-fold the top triangular flap down.

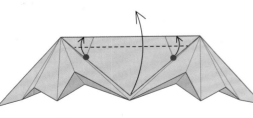

16 Valley-fold the triangular flap up. The correct amount can be determined by placing the ends of the indicated creases (red dots) upon the top folded edge.

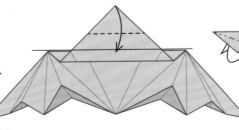

17 Valley-fold the top corner down, just a bit below the level at the black line, which represents the level of the hidden folded edge, behind.

18 Valley-fold the corner up at the level of the hidden folded edge. Fold corner down to touch the middle of the folded edge, below. Mountain-fold the indicated edges under as far as possible.

19 Your paper should look like this.

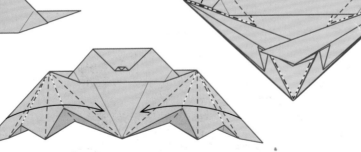

20 Use the pleats in the wings to close and flatten the model.

21 Mountain-fold along the edges of the wings, from their outward corners down to the creases on the body. Move these mountain-folded edges of the wings up to the top corners of the head, valley-folding between to make the body plump.

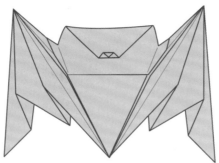

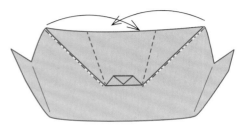

22 Open the wings, slightly.

23 Mountain-fold along the cut edges of the top layer of paper on the head, stopping at the mouth corners. Fold the top corners of the head over each other and raise them straight up for the ears.

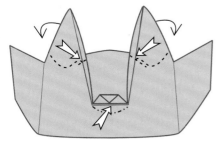

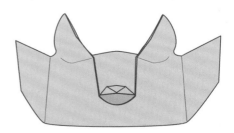

24 Twist the ears to face forward.

Open the mouth — you may use the point of a skewer or pen to do this. Be creative and form the bat's expression with these folds.

25 Detail of the head.

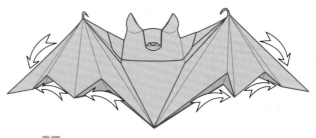

Curl the thumbs inward.

26 Open the wings wide.

27 Make graceful curves in the outer edges and the scalloped underline of the wings.

28 The Happy Good-luck Bat

The Alexander Aztec Swallowtail Butterfly

designed by Michael G. LaFosse

LESSON: WET-FOLDING WITH DUO PAPERS

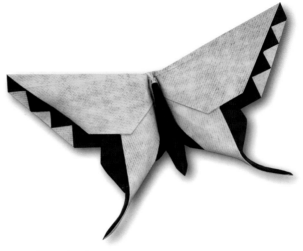

Tiger swallowtail butterflies were always my favorite, and when Michael began to explore variations of his origami butterfly design system, I was particularly taken by the beauty of a version that he later dubbed the "Alexander Swallowtail." At about the same time, I had been teaching my fancy variation of the three-piece, six-facet box by Molly Kahn, and I found that by fan-folding the inner flap to the outside, my students had a much easier time assembling the three pieces. I named it the "Fiesta Box" because the resulting triangular spots reminded me of so many popular decorations south of the border. It didn't take long for Michael to adopt fan-folded, triangular spots to grace the wings of his origami butterflies. We happened to be working on updating our video butterfly lessons, and this version, sporting my favorite swallowtail wing treatment, was realized. As with my Fiesta Box, this butterfly looks great when folded from thicker Japanese duo-color foil. If you use fancy papers instead, it is best to wet fold a pasted duo-color laminate.

● Back coating is an essential technique that separates the more serious origami artists from the casual folders. Back coating does much more than make thicker paper, or make paper that has a different desired color on each side. It can do both of those things, but it also allows the artist to create a much stronger laminate that includes an important layer of internal size between the two sheets. This methylcellulose gel is an archival, water-soluble adhesive that lubricates the fibers and allows the layers to slide imperceptibly as the model is folded and shaped. It sets when dry to retain the desired pose or position. Back coating fine papers with methylcellulose provides exceptional strength during complex folding, allows more artful shaping possibilities, and produces a more durable final product.

● **It is easier to back coat the two different papers if one is slightly larger than the other. Most laminates dry properly when at least a ¾" margin about the perimeter can be pasted onto the drying board. (This means that you should trim one piece to be 1½" shorter in each dimension.)**

● After trimming, use a spray bottle and a brush to add moisture evenly to both sides of each sheet that you will be laminating. Add methylcellulose to the largest sheet only. Brush the adhesive along one diagonal, and then from the center to each of the remaining corners. Working the adhesive with the brush from the center to the edges allows the paper to "grow" as the cellulose fibers swell and relax with the addition of the moisture and adhesive. More methylcellulose will require more drying time. An uneven coat will dry unevenly and pucker, so work the layer long enough with the brush to ensure an even coating. If the gel is adjusted to the proper consistency, it will relax on the surface and look glossy and even. Too thin, and it will disappear into the fibers. Too thick, and the blobs won't spread out and level into a glossy glaze.

● **Add the second moistened sheet, centered on top of the applied gel. You might want to have somebody help you by holding two of the corners. Lower one end first, and gently adhere the lowered sheet onto the wet adhesive. Using a wide, dry brush, work any trapped air bubbles to the edges where they can be released.**

● Tear a ¾" x 1½" "tongue" (or gate) of scrap paper to lay across the gooey perimeter. This will prevent the paper from sticking to the backer (drying surface) at that one spot, where a knife can later be inserted to release the pasted perimeter from the backer. Transfer the wet laminate by flipping it onto the backing surface. Allow the paper to dry. As moisture leaves, the sheets will shrink and tighten.

● **When dry, release the paper from the backer by inserting a knife at the "tongue" (or gate). Trim squares for your project!**

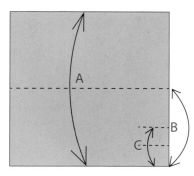

1 Begin with the "wrong" side up. (A) Valley-fold in half, bottom edge to top edge. Unfold. (B) Valley-fold the bottom edge to the center crease, making only a short pinch mark at the right edge of the paper. Unfold. (C) Valley-fold the bottom edge to the bottom pinch mark, making a new pinch mark. Unfold.

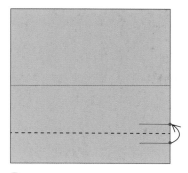

2 Lay the bottom pinch mark upon the one above to valley-fold the distance between them in half.

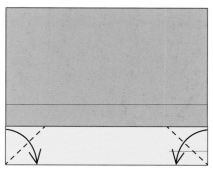

3 Valley-fold each of the two free corners of the bottom flap to align their short edges with the bottom edge.

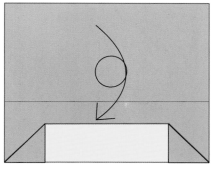

4 Your paper should look like this. Turn over, top to bottom.

5 Valley-fold the bottom edge to the crease, making only a short pinch mark at the right edge of the paper. Unfold.

6 Valley-fold the bottom edge to the pinch mark, folding the full length of the paper. Unfold.

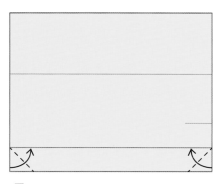

7 Valley-fold the bottom corners up, aligning their short edges to the crease.

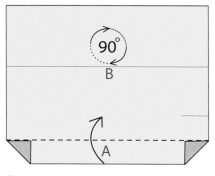

8 (A) Valley-fold the bottom flap up. Rotate the paper 90 degrees clockwise.

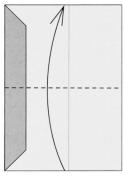

9 Valley-fold in half, bottom short edge to top short edge.

10 Squash-fold the smaller right half of the model.

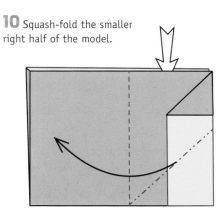

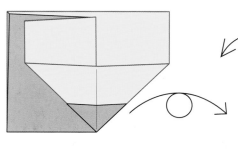

11 Your paper should look like this. Turn over from left to right.

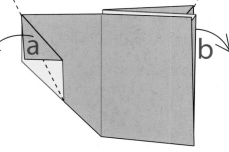

12 Pull out the flaps marked "a" and "b" and valley-fold to flatten.

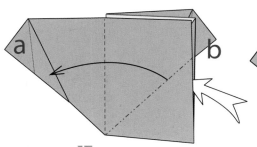

13 Squash-fold.

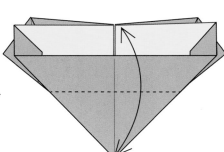

14 Valley-fold the bottom corner to the top of the split. Unfold.

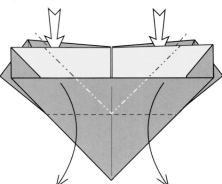

15 Squash-fold the top left and right quadrants, hinging at the horizontal center crease. Look ahead for the result.

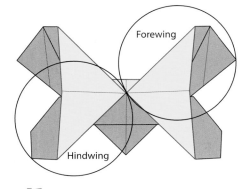

16 Your paper should look like this. This is one of my many origami butterfly system basic forms. Hundreds of new "species" of origami butterflies can be developed from these bases. Let's go on to refine the forewings and hindwings for the Alexander Aztec Swallowtail.

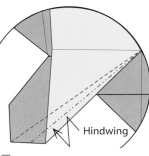

17 Valley- and mountain-fold the lower edge of the hindwings, forming fan pleats.

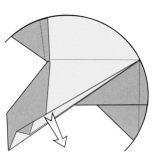

18 Unfold the pleats.

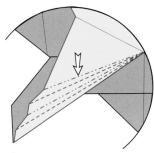

19 Pull up the top layer of the hindwings and mountain- and valley-fold along the creases to collapse the fan.

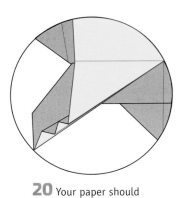

20 Your paper should look like this.

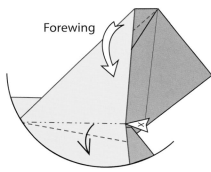

21 Sharply mountain-fold the horizontal center crease, indicated here with an "X" arrowhead, and move it downward, pulling the top edge of the forewing down with it. Valley-fold under the mountain fold and at the top of the wing to flatten the shape. Look ahead at the next drawing for the result.

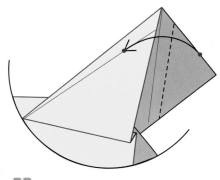

22 Valley-fold the square-cornered flaps over the forewings, aligning the top edge of the flaps with their associated crease.

23 Valley- and mountain-fold the remnant of the flaps that overlap the topmost layers of the forewings, making a two-colored border of triangles. Inside-reverse-fold the indicated corners at the outside base of the forewings.

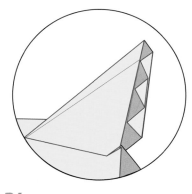

24 The forewings should look like this.

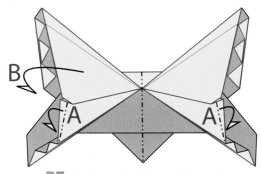

25 (A) Mountain-fold the indicated vertical edges behind the top layer of each hindwing. (B) Mountain-fold the butterfly in half, wing to wing.

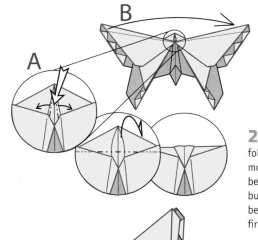

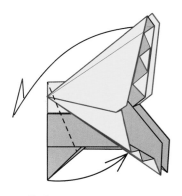

26 Valley-fold the left edge at an angle, pivoting at the top left corner and making the bottom corner touch the trailing edge of the top hindwing. Allow the full wing at the back to swing into view on the left.

27 (A) Form the head: Squash-fold the center rib flat, then mountain-fold the flattened flap behind. (B) Gently fold the butterfly in half, wing to wing, being careful not to press too firmly at the head, lest it tear.

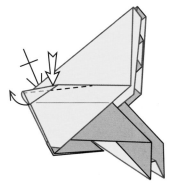

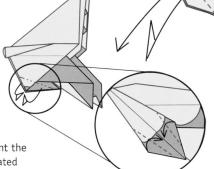

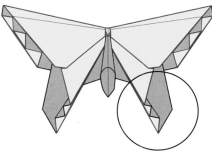

28 Adjust the head angle to prevent the paper from splitting: Push the indicated folded edges, front and back, down simultaneously, making the bottom edge of the head jut out slightly. Valley-fold firmly to flatten the newly formed edges.

29 Taper the underside of the abdomen by mountain-folding the short, hind edges inside the model.

30 Valley-fold each wing down, folding between the points marked with "X" arrowheads, spanning from the top of the head to the wing-locking point near the abdomen.

31 Open and set the wings, as shown. Hindwing folding detail to follow.

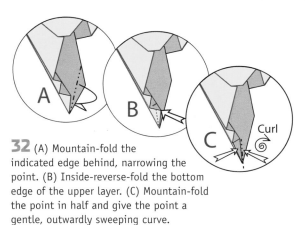

32 (A) Mountain-fold the indicated edge behind, narrowing the point. (B) Inside-reverse-fold the bottom edge of the upper layer. (C) Mountain-fold the point in half and give the point a gentle, outwardly sweeping curve.

Takeaways: Metamorphosis in Origami

Michael is fond of calling origami a "metamorphic art form." A sheet of paper is transformed, only by folding, into a sculptural piece with enhanced beauty or meaning. With its papery wings and metamorphic life cycle, what better subject could there be to represent origami than the butterfly? This example, the Alexander Aztec Swallowtail, is only one of hundreds of origami butterfly designs that Michael has created, and they are all based upon a handful of folding routines that constitute Michael's creative origami butterfly designing efforts. These folding routines may be mixed and matched in thousands of ways to produce new "species" of butterflies. Since 1992, I have helped him explain and share his origami butterfly design system in several videos, books and kits, and I consider it his most important "gift" to the world of origami because Michael's base is fun, simple and quick, yet it allows stunningly creative variation. In that way, it reminds me of *Senbazuru*, the first published "system" of creating "thousands" of interesting variations of Japanese origami cranes. I (Richard Alexander), am particularly proud that Michael named this variation of his origami butterfly for me.

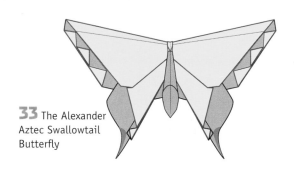

33 The Alexander Aztec Swallowtail Butterfly

The Wedding Orchid

designed by Michael G. LaFosse

LESSON: MULTI-PIECE FOLDING AND TRANSPORTATION

Michael was encouraged by the popular response to his origami butterfly design system. He wanted to follow up with a similar approach to folding a variety of orchids that would be manageable to the average folder. While he has designed single square orchid blossoms, their huge variation and complexity seemed better served by a multi-piece approach. Compound origami models allowed him to create different types of orchid blossoms with interlocking (and interchangeable) components. While he was working on these designs he was asked to recommend an origami orchid design that could be folded by a recently engaged couple for their upcoming special day. The result: The Wedding Orchid! It is a three-piece construction, an example of multi-piece or compound origami. (Although it is quite possible to design a complex origami flowering plant that is folded from a single, uncut square, the process often requires a costly compromise in elegance.)

In this case, each square contributes one sepal and one petal. Fold two 2½" squares of back coated paper, as a mirror image set of the same design. A third square provides the striking splash of color at the center (folded from another 2½" square of "duo" paper). The third square is folded quite differently, which enables it to lock into the components on each side.

Takeaways: The Concert

Because compound origami uses multiple sheets, each folded to participate as one part of the whole composition, no other style of origami reminds me as much of the orchestra: each component individually accomplished, yet each may be a frustratingly unintelligible fraction until it is united upon performance in concert with others. Each piece must be folded precisely for a good fit. Many viewers won't even realize that there are individual parts.

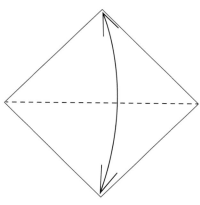

1 Let's first learn how to fold the Petal/Sepal Unit. Begin with the "wrong" side up if using paper colored differently on each side. Valley-fold in half diagonally, bottom corner to top. Unfold.

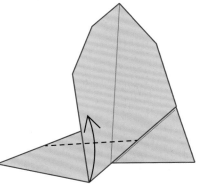

2 Turn over, bottom to top.

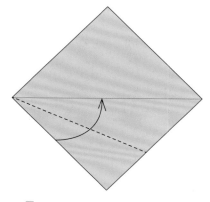

3 Valley-fold the bottom left edge to the horizontal crease.

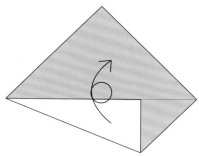

4 Turn over, bottom to top.

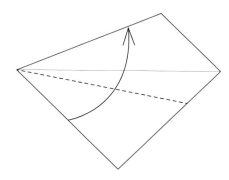

5 Valley-fold the bottom left edge to the top folded edge.

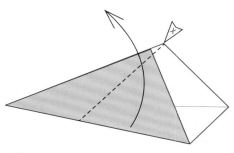

6 Valley-fold a portion of the right side up. Be sure to make your fold intersect the top corner, marked here with the "X" arrow. Look ahead at the next diagram for the shape.

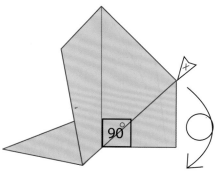

7 Your paper should look like this. Notice that the vertical crease is set 90 degrees to the bottom horizontal right side edge. You may experiment with other angles. Turn over, top to bottom.

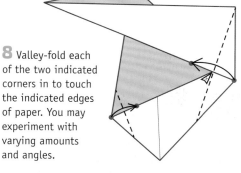

8 Valley-fold each of the two indicated corners in to touch the indicated edges of paper. You may experiment with varying amounts and angles.

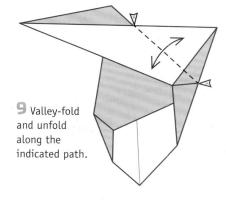

9 Valley-fold and unfold along the indicated path.

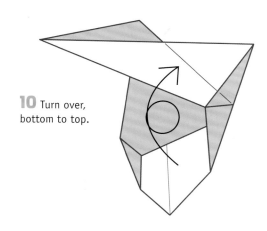

10 Turn over, bottom to top.

11 Open the sepal by valley-folding the bottom flap up. Look ahead at the next diagram for the shape.

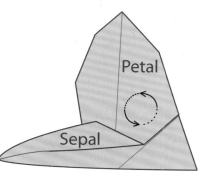

Petal

Sepal

12 The completed Petal/Sepal Unit. Rotate to view the petal at top left and the sepal at bottom left.

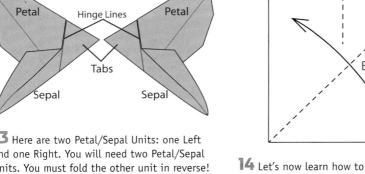

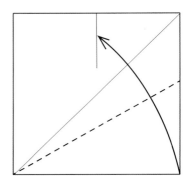

13 Here are two Petal/Sepal Units: one Left and one Right. You will need two Petal/Sepal Units. You must fold the other unit in reverse! Notice the tab and hinge line on each unit. You will use these structures to attach the units to the central, Sepal/Lip Unit.

14 Let's now learn how to fold the Sepal/Lip Unit. Begin with the "wrong" side up if using paper colored differently on each side. (A) Valley-fold the top edge in half. Unfold. (B) Valley-fold in half diagonally, bottom right corner to top left. Unfold.

15 Valley-fold the bottom right corner up to touch the top crease, while making sure the fold being formed intersects the bottom left corner.

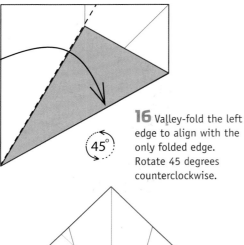

16 Valley-fold the left edge to align with the only folded edge. Rotate 45 degrees counterclockwise.

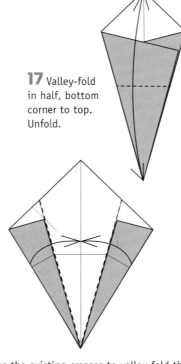

17 Valley-fold in half, bottom corner to top. Unfold.

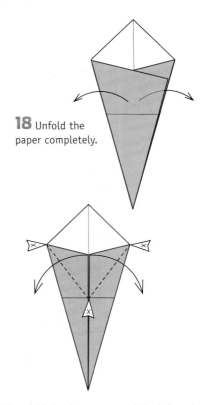

18 Unfold the paper completely.

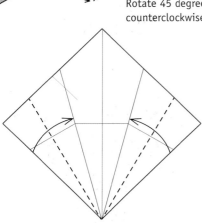

19 The crease pattern in your paper should look like this. Valley-fold the bottom left and right edges to align with their nearest radial crease.

20 Use the existing creases to valley-fold the left and right folded edges to the vertical center.

21 Valley-fold the free corners of the left and right triangular flaps out. Use the indicated corners and crease, marked with "X" arrows, to obtain the correct shape and size for each.

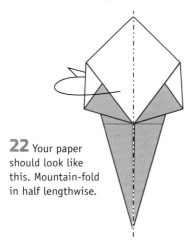

22 Your paper should look like this. Mountain-fold in half lengthwise.

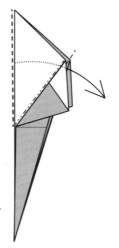

23 Inside-reverse-fold the top triangular flap.

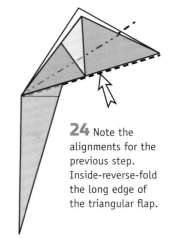

24 Note the alignments for the previous step. Inside-reverse-fold the long edge of the triangular flap.

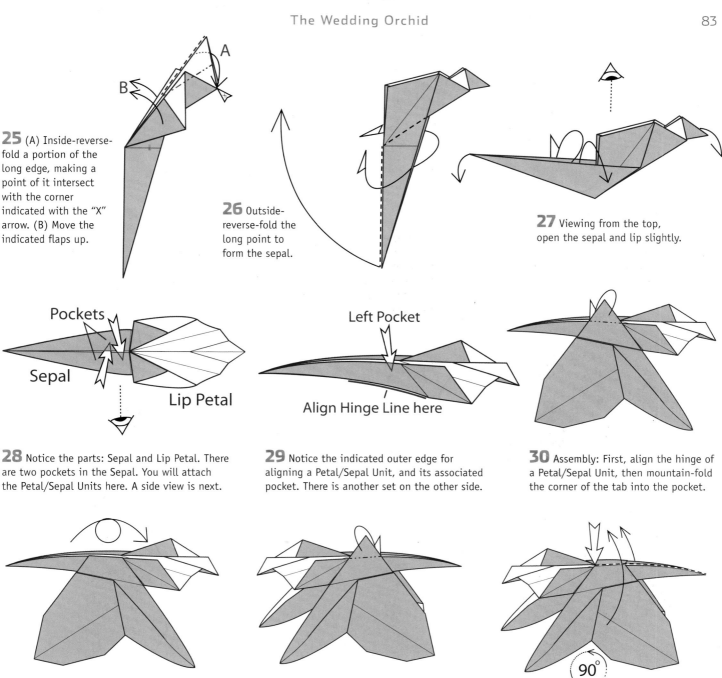

25 (A) Inside-reverse-fold a portion of the long edge, making a point of it intersect with the corner indicated with the "X" arrow. (B) Move the indicated flaps up.

26 Outside-reverse-fold the long point to form the sepal.

27 Viewing from the top, open the sepal and lip slightly.

Pockets

Sepal

Lip Petal

28 Notice the parts: Sepal and Lip Petal. There are two pockets in the Sepal. You will attach the Petal/Sepal Units here. A side view is next.

Left Pocket

Align Hinge Line here

29 Notice the indicated outer edge for aligning a Petal/Sepal Unit, and its associated pocket. There is another set on the other side.

30 Assembly: First, align the hinge of a Petal/Sepal Unit, then mountain-fold the corner of the tab into the pocket.

31 One Petal/Sepal Unit attached. Turn to the other side.

32 Attach the other Petal/Sepal unit.

33 Push down at the center and valley-fold the center sepal to set the shape and further secure the Petal/Sepal Units. Rotate to view.

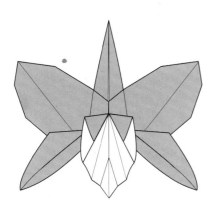

34 The Wedding Orchid

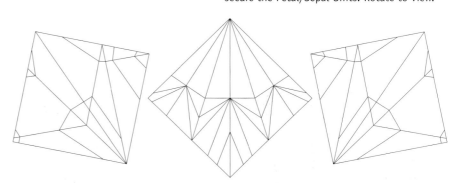

Here are three crease patterns, representing the left, center, and right units of the Wedding Orchid, respectively.

Enough of this Cat!

designed by Michael G. LaFosse

LESSON: CHOOSING PROPORTIONS, IMPACTS OF VARIATION

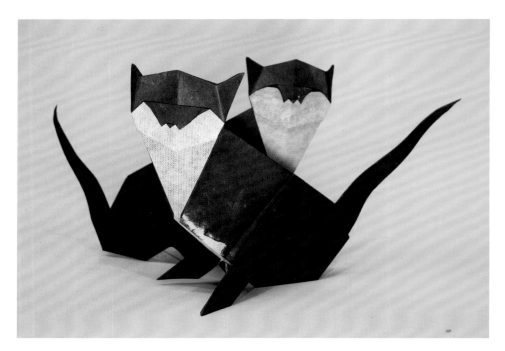

This rascal is fun to fold and to pose in different ways, to explore a wide range of attitudes. Michael prefers the countenance of the abstract seated cat, to that of so many standing four-legged counterparts. This étude is designed to have you explore different ways to convey your cat's mood or personality with subtle folds: tweaking the ears, adjusting its posture, and exploring the variety of expression on its face. These all work together to convey a cat's mood. A cat also uses its tail to express emotions, so have some fun with experimentation. Your choices will determine if it appears relaxed and friendly, or threatening. (It may be the only cat to ever obey you!) Folded as diagrammed makes an adult cat. What proportions could you change to produce a kitten? It's more involved than just selecting a smaller square — it also has to do with the line of the back, the proportion of the head to the body, and other factors. A crimp placed between the back of the neck and the arm changes both the attitude and the proportion of the head to the body. This is just one way to make your cat appear younger.

Also try different textures of papers to match this model to your vision. Some cats are slender and sleek. Others aren't: My Aunt Katie had a monster cat named Smokey, who terrorized and attacked any visitors. For Smokey, I would fold a big square of rough-surfaced, gray art paper (perhaps roughing it up even more with a kitchen scrubber). My favorite cat was Zeek, a half-Siamese vocal companion, so be sure to give him an open mouth, because Zeek loved to speak!

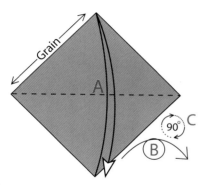

1 Begin with the paper right side up, diamond-wise, and with the grain running parallel to the top left edge. (A) Valley-fold diagonally in half. Unfold. (B) Turn over, left to right. (C) Rotate 90 degrees clockwise.

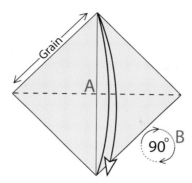

2 (A) Valley-fold diagonally in half. Unfold. (B) Rotate 90 degrees clockwise.

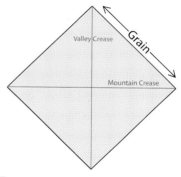

3 Check to see that the horizontal and vertical creases are mountain and valley respectively, and that the grain is running parallel to the top right edge.

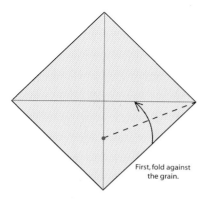

4 Valley-fold the bottom right edge to align with the horizontal crease. Stop the fold at the vertical center crease. Here, you have the chance to employ both hands and focus your attention on coaxing the paper to a fine point at the right corner.

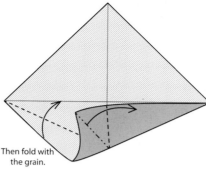

5 Mountain-fold the center square corner in half and pivot it to the right. Valley-fold the bottom left edge to align with the horizontal crease. Here, your hands have multiple tasks. Nevertheless, you will notice how easily this set of folds takes shape. This is no accident! Your careful preparation of orienting the valley crease vertically, and the grain parallel to the bottom left edge, combine to condition the paper to easily accept this otherwise tricky maneuver.

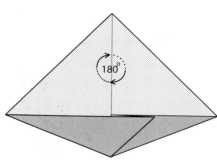

6 Rotate the paper 180 degrees.

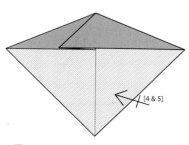

7 Repeat steps 4 and 5 on the bottom half of the paper.

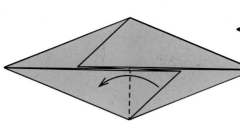

8 Valley-fold the bottom flap to the left.

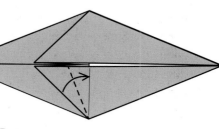

9 Valley-fold the longest edge of the flap to align with the vertical crease.

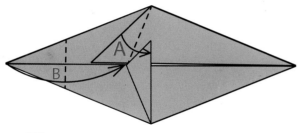

10 (A) Valley-fold the longest edge of the top flap to align with the vertical folded edge of the bottom flap. (B) Valley-fold the left corner to the obtuse corner of the folded flaps.

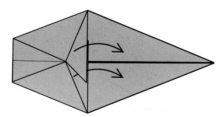

11 Unfold the top and bottom flaps to make them point to the right.

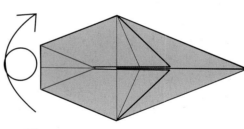

12 Notice and remember the position of the left-side triangular flap. Turn the paper over, bottom to top.

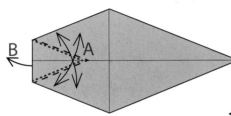

13 (A) Valley-fold and unfold along the top and bottom outlines of the hidden, left-side triangular flap. (B) Unfold the hidden triangular flap out and to the left.

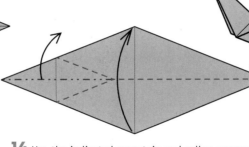

14 Use the indicated mountain and valley creases to inside-reverse-fold the left corner upward, valley-folding the paper in half lengthwise.

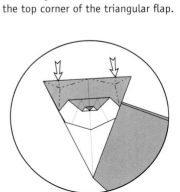

15 Your paper should look like this. (A) Valley-fold the top layer of the left end of the paper upward and to the right. (B) Valley-fold the longest edge of the triangular flap to align with the vertical center crease. Repeat on the flap behind. These will become the cat's front legs. (C) Rotate the paper 45 degrees clockwise.

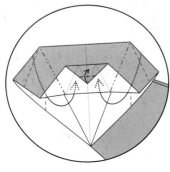

16 Open the top layers of the rhombus form and move the top corner to the bottom, folding the area in half and forming a pentagon. This area will become the head. Folding details for the head follow.

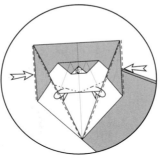

17 Valley-fold the bottom corner of the pentagon up to the middle of the top edge.

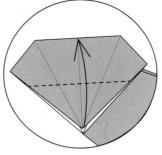

18 Valley-fold down about one-third of the top corner of the triangular flap.

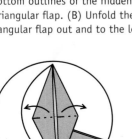

19 Valley-fold up about one-third of the square corner of the topmost triangular flap. Inside-reverse-fold the sides of the head. Look at the next drawing for the shape

20 Valley-fold the square corner of the topmost triangular flap down for a nose. Inside-reverse-fold the left and right flaps behind the triangular-shaped layer of the neck. Mountain-fold the left and right corners of the head to form the chin.

21 Mountain- and valley-fold the top left and right corners to form the ears and to round the top of the head.

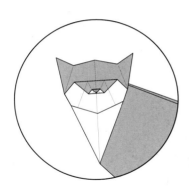

22 The completed cat's head.

23 Valley-fold the bottom right-side corner up, folding at the level of the bottom edge of the cat's front legs, to prepare the paper for a tail.

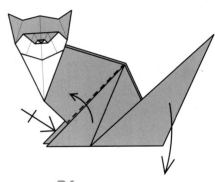

24 Valley-fold the cat's legs over. Unfold the tail flap.

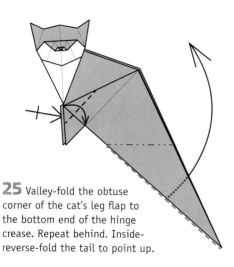

25 Valley-fold the obtuse corner of the cat's leg flap to the bottom end of the hinge crease. Repeat behind. Inside-reverse-fold the tail to point up.

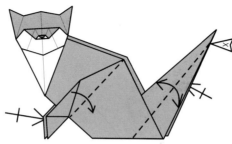

26 Valley-fold the cat's legs down. Valley-fold the long, outside edge of the tail to nearly align with the tail's spine line. Notice the indication to stop the fold short of the tip. Repeat on the other side. Unfold.

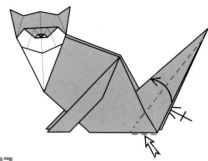

27 Inside-reverse-fold the front and back flaps on the tail.

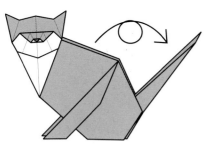

28 At this point, you may be satisfied and have had enough of this cat. If not, turn over, left to right to learn how to change the shape of and to lock the back closed.

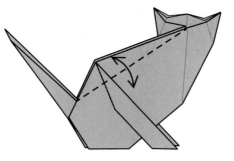

29 Valley-fold the corner of the topmost layer down. Make the fold span the base of the tail up to the neck joint. Unfold.

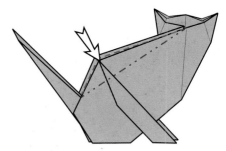

30 Push the corner inside, sinking the triangular flap to form a pocket.

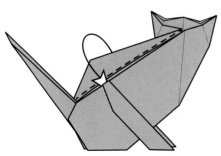

31 Valley-fold the exposed corner tightly inside the pocket, closing the back.

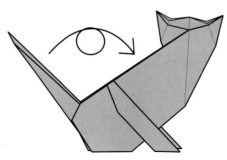

32 Turn over.

33 Gently curve the tail.

34 You may be satisfied with Enough of this Cat. If this is not quite enough of this cat for you, follow along to add a pair of hind feet, and some color-change paws!

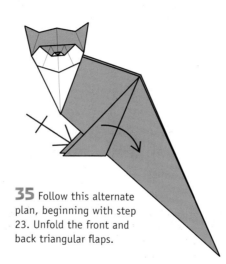

35 Follow this alternate plan, beginning with step 23. Unfold the front and back triangular flaps.

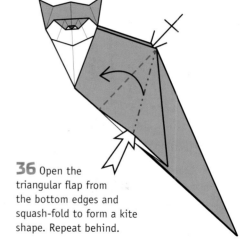

36 Open the triangular flap from the bottom edges and squash-fold to form a kite shape. Repeat behind.

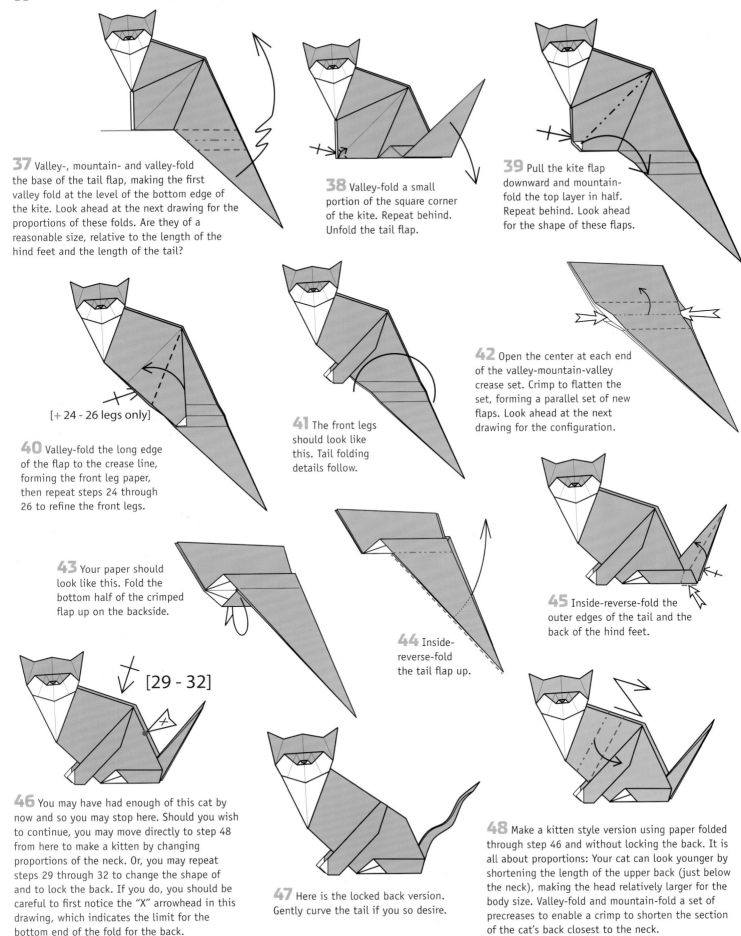

37 Valley-, mountain- and valley-fold the base of the tail flap, making the first valley fold at the level of the bottom edge of the kite. Look ahead at the next drawing for the proportions of these folds. Are they of a reasonable size, relative to the length of the hind feet and the length of the tail?

38 Valley-fold a small portion of the square corner of the kite. Repeat behind. Unfold the tail flap.

39 Pull the kite flap downward and mountain-fold the top layer in half. Repeat behind. Look ahead for the shape of these flaps.

[+ 24 - 26 legs only]

40 Valley-fold the long edge of the flap to the crease line, forming the front leg paper, then repeat steps 24 through 26 to refine the front legs.

41 The front legs should look like this. Tail folding details follow.

42 Open the center at each end of the valley-mountain-valley crease set. Crimp to flatten the set, forming a parallel set of new flaps. Look ahead at the next drawing for the configuration.

43 Your paper should look like this. Fold the bottom half of the crimped flap up on the backside.

44 Inside-reverse-fold the tail flap up.

45 Inside-reverse-fold the outer edges of the tail and the back of the hind feet.

[29 - 32]

46 You may have had enough of this cat by now and so you may stop here. Should you wish to continue, you may move directly to step 48 from here to make a kitten by changing proportions of the neck. Or, you may repeat steps 29 through 32 to change the shape of and to lock the back. If you do, you should be careful to first notice the "X" arrowhead in this drawing, which indicates the limit for the bottom end of the fold for the back.

47 Here is the locked back version. Gently curve the tail if you so desire.

48 Make a kitten style version using paper folded through step 46 and without locking the back. It is all about proportions: Your cat can look younger by shortening the length of the upper back (just below the neck), making the head relatively larger for the body size. Valley-fold and mountain-fold a set of precreases to enable a crimp to shorten the section of the cat's back closest to the neck.

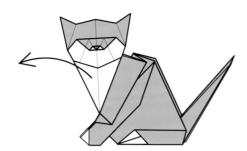

49 Your paper should look like this. Pull the pleats open.

50 Using the pre-creases that you just made, crimp the model inside to shorten the length of the neck and the back.

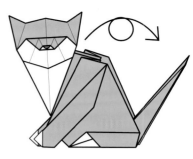

51 Your paper should look like this. Turn over left to right.

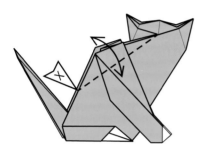

52 Valley-fold the top layers down at the top to the back, from the head, to the "X" arrow. Unfold.

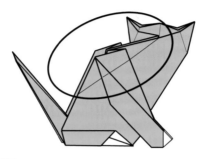

53 Let's take a closer look at the back.

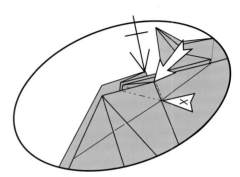

54 Inside-reverse-fold the indicated corner, pivoting at the crease line formed in step 52, indicated by the "X" arrow. Repeat behind (and by the same amount).

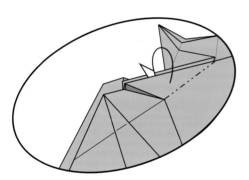

55 Mountain-fold the indicated flap inside.

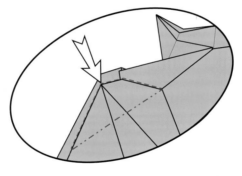

56 Sink the flap (form a pocket), using the indicated crease line from step 52.

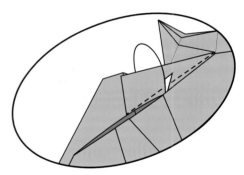

57 Valley-fold the indicated flap inside the back-neck area.

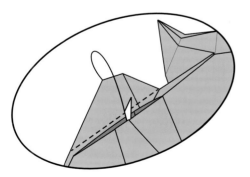

58 Fold and tuck the indicated flap into the open pocket formed by the sink in step 56, locking the back.

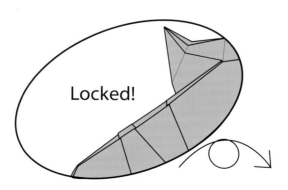

Locked!

59 The flap is locked. Turn the model over, left to right.

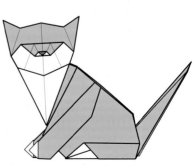

60 By now, you must have folded Enough of this Cat!

The Leatherback Sea Turtle

designed by Michael G. LaFosse

LESSON: PRE-PAINTING AND WET FOLDING 90-POUND
COTTON WATERCOLOR PAPER

cotton rag watercolor paper, and this choice works well for such a structural model. Watercolor paper contains an additive similar to gelatin, which makes the paper stiff when it is dry. This helps to control the migration of watercolor paints and pigments, and so we decided to color the paper with a mottled blue pattern before folding the model. The additive is water-reversible and so the paper folds more easily when it is slightly moistened. Although these papers are relatively thick, the cotton fibers are still quite compressible.

Why not color your watercolor paper to exactly the appearance you desire? It is not difficult, and it is quite fun! If you want your work to last, remember to use the best fine artist-quality pigments, papers and materials that you can afford. For this project, use the tools in the photo: spray bottle, brush, archival ink and a dish!

These massive turtles' elongated, ridged, teardrop-shaped shell provides an exciting form to approximate in folded paper. Smooth and rounded turtles require big compromises for origami artists, but this species sports structurally reinforcing ribs that are highly satisfying because they are so doable with folding. As SCUBA divers, we love to catch a glimpse of any sea turtles, but we must admit that we would be both highly excited and at least a little bit frightened if we came across a huge, ten-foot long leatherback sea turtle. We prefer to fold this model from 90-pound (fairly lightweight) commercial, cold press 90%

Here is a selection of tools and materials for painting the watercolor paper. Paints may be mixed in a flat-bottomed glass or plastic pan. Thin with water to make the paint easy to spread. Place protective materials under and around the watercolor paper to prevent paint from getting onto surfaces that you need to keep clean. Repeat the process to "relax" the paper.

Materials:

- Acrylic paints (Blue and Black) plus water for mixing and thinning
- Paint mixing tray
- Three-inch-wide acrylic paintbrush
- Spray bottle filled with water

- Wide, soft brush or cloth for spreading water on paper
- Paper towels
- 80- or 90-pound weight rag content watercolor paper, trimmed to the largest possible square, approximately 22 inches (56 cm), from the full-size sheet.

Spray water generously over the entire surface of one side of the watercolor paper.

Use a soft dry brush or cloth to spread the water evenly across the paper.

Apply paint with a wide acrylic paintbrush, brushing parallel to a side of the square and in the same direction, creating a streaky grain.

Work quickly to coat the entire sheet so that the entire sheet will be freshly wet.

Fold a piece of paper towel into a pointed shape and touch repeatedly over the area of the freshly painted surface to make a pattern of small white spots.

Let the paper dry completely.

Paint a border of color on the backside of the sheet. Let dry completely.

There is a huge Leatherback Sea Turtle specimen, preserved and mounted at the entrance to the Museum of Comparative Zoology at Harvard University. The Boston Malacological (mollusk) Club meets monthly in the classroom near where this mounted creature has been proudly on display for decades. Professor George Buckley says that it was one of the last huge individuals ever seen. Even the relatively tiny, 2-foot "babies" seen occasionally in the Gulf of Maine are quite rare sightings today. A few of these join the more common green sea turtles in strandings on the inner curl of Cape Cod almost every year, especially if bitter cold weather comes early and catches them during their migration back to warmer southern waters.

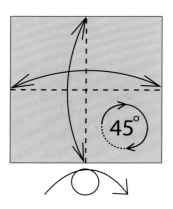

1 Begin right side up. Valley-fold in half edge to edge both ways, unfolding after each. Turn over and rotate 45 degrees.

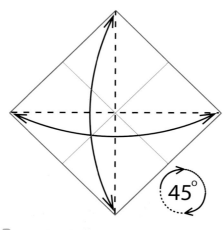

2 Valley-fold in half diagonally both ways, unfolding after each. Rotate 45 degrees.

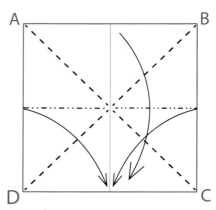

3 Collapse the square into a layered triangular shape, open at the bottom. Note carefully the position of the corners and the layering.

4 Your paper should look like this.

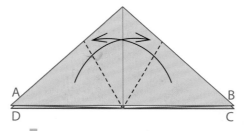

5 Valley-fold the left (A) and right (B) corner flaps to overlap in equal thirds, with flap B on top.

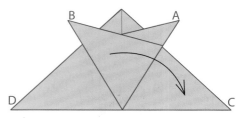

6 Your paper should look like this. Return flap B to the bottom right.

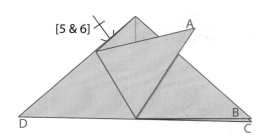

7 Repeat steps 5 and 6 on the other side. Be sure to organize corners C and D correctly, then return the paper to the position shown in step 8.

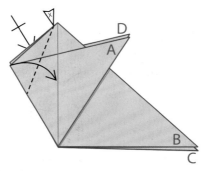

8 Valley-fold the top left obtuse corner to touch the vertical center crease, folding at an angle that will leave the top corner slightly blunted. Notice where the fold stops at the top, marked by the "X" arrowhead. Repeat behind.

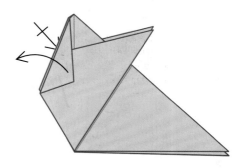

9 Your paper should look like this. Unfold the front and back flaps.

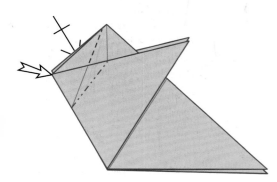

10 Inside-reverse-fold the front and back flaps.

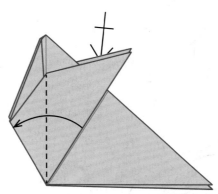

11 Valley-fold the top triangular flap of the right side to the left. Repeat behind.

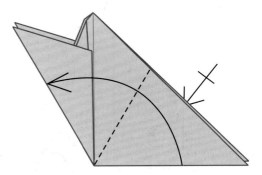

12 Use the existing valley creases to fold the large triangular flaps over, one in the front and the other in the back.

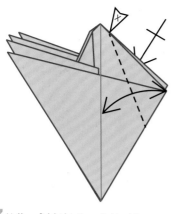

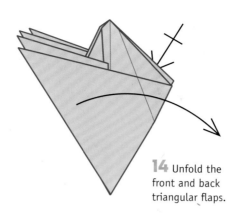

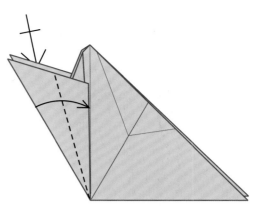

13 Valley-fold the top right obtuse corner to touch the vertical center crease, folding at an angle that will leave the top corner slightly blunted. Notice where the fold stops at the top, marked by the "X" arrowhead. Unfold. Repeat behind.

14 Unfold the front and back triangular flaps.

15 Valley-fold the left edge of the left-side triangular flap to align with the vertical right edge. Repeat behind.

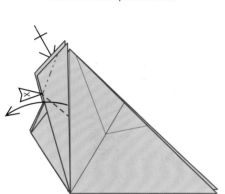

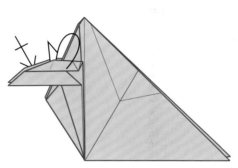

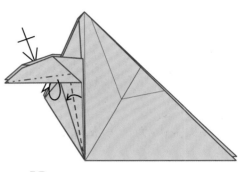

16 Move the top end of the triangular flap to the left, pivoting at the point indicated by the "X" arrowhead, and squash-fold, forming the front flippers. Repeat behind.

17 Wrap the top layer of the flipper over to the other side. Repeat behind.

18 Mountain-fold the bottom edge of the flipper up and under while valley-folding the vertical right edge of the associated lower flap to the left edge. Repeat behind.

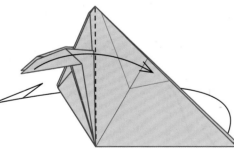

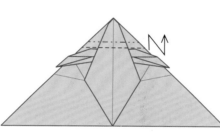

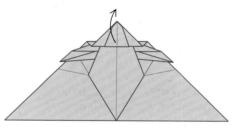

19 Move the top left half of the paper to the right and the back right half to the left.

20 Your paper should look like this. Valley- and mountain-fold the top corner, to prepare for folding the head and neck.

21 Your paper should look like this. Unfold.

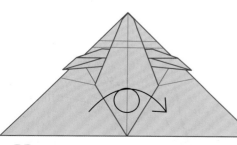

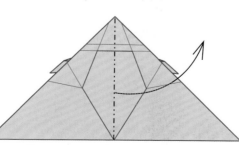

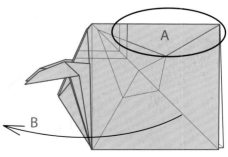

22 Turn over, left to right.

23 First, notice the pentagonally-shaped crease outline, highlighted in red. This area will become the dorsal shell. Lift the top layer of paper up and to the right, mountain-folding it in half. Look ahead to the next drawing for the shape.

24 (A) Install mountain and valley creases on the dorsal surface of the shell that are detailed in step 25. (B) Move the top right layer to the left, returning the dorsal shell to the center.

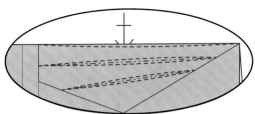

25 Detail for step 24-A: Pinch triple crease sets — valley, mountain, valley — that span from the front of the dorsal shell to the back. You should install five sets: one at the top center and two each, on the front and the back sides of the model.

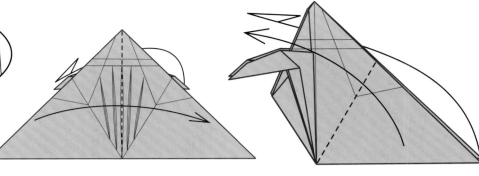

26 Move the top left half of the paper to the right and the back right half to the left.

27 Use the existing valley creases to fold the large triangular flaps over, one in the front and the other in the back.

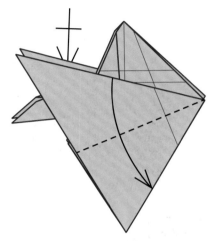

28 Valley-fold the top edge of the triangular flap to the bottom right edge. Repeat behind.

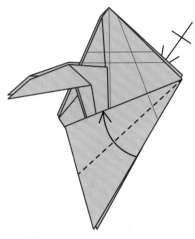

29 Valley-fold the bottom right edge of the triangular flap to the top edge. Repeat behind.

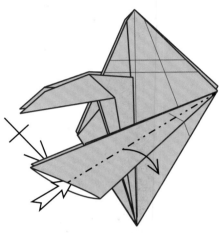

30 Squash-fold the topmost triangular flap to form the hind flipper. Repeat behind.

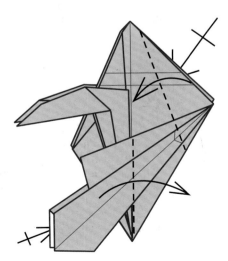

31 Use the existing creases to valley-fold the top right flap to touch the center crease. Repeat behind. Valley-fold the flipper along the vertical center, to the left. Repeat behind.

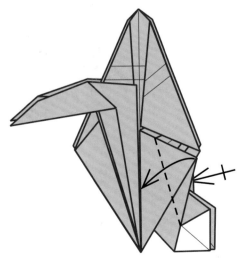

32 Valley-fold the indicated corner over to touch the vertical center line, making the fold stop at the overlapping layers of the hind flipper. Repeat behind.

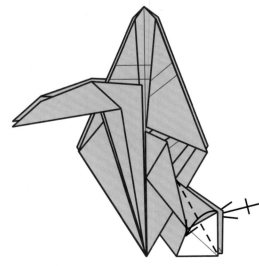

33 Valley-fold the outer corner of the flipper over, making a single folded edge that spans from the top limit to the bottom corner. Repeat behind.

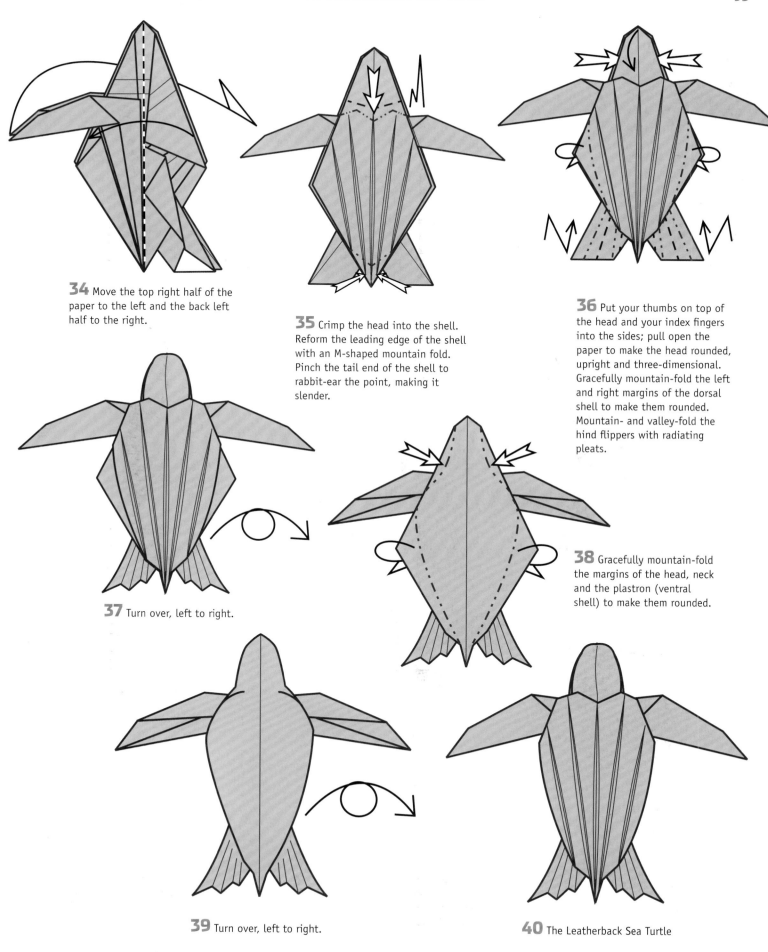

34 Move the top right half of the paper to the left and the back left half to the right.

35 Crimp the head into the shell. Reform the leading edge of the shell with an M-shaped mountain fold. Pinch the tail end of the shell to rabbit-ear the point, making it slender.

36 Put your thumbs on top of the head and your index fingers into the sides; pull open the paper to make the head rounded, upright and three-dimensional. Gracefully mountain-fold the left and right margins of the dorsal shell to make them rounded. Mountain- and valley-fold the hind flippers with radiating pleats.

37 Turn over, left to right.

38 Gracefully mountain-fold the margins of the head, neck and the plastron (ventral shell) to make them rounded.

39 Turn over, left to right.

40 The Leatherback Sea Turtle

Acknowledgments

We wish to acknowledge Anne LaVin for her generous contribution of her elegant origami squirrel design. We thank our friends at the Honolulu Museum of Art, Education Director, Aaron Padilla; and hand paper maker / artist, Allison Roscoe, who helped to make our origami art contribution to the exhibit, "Less=More" at Spalding House such a grand success. The Kondo and Miyatake families contributed in countless ways and over many years. We must also acknowledge the inspiring works of the late Akira Yoshizawa, each skillfully infused with the spirit and the love of the artist through his talented hands. We also owe our gratitude to the late Lillian Oppenheimer, the Grandmother of Origami in the USA, whose views about teaching still resonate with hundreds of others like us who continue to share origami with youngsters of every age. We thank Elaine, Sidney and Donna Koretsky of Carriage House Paper, for helping us gain command of paper making fibers and pigments through their decades of research, publications, workshops and materials. Finally, we thank our steady and intrepid editor at Tuttle Publishing, Jon Steever, for persevering with us through so many original origami and folded art publishing productions.

Richard L. Alexander and Michael G. LaFosse,
Origamido Studio

Published by Tuttle Publishing, an imprint of Periplus Editions (HK) Ltd.

www.tuttlepublishing.com

Copyright © 2016 by Michael G. LaFosse and Richard L. Alexander

Library of Congress Cataloging-in-Publication Data

Names: LaFosse, Michael G., author. | Alexander, Richard L., 1953- author.
Title: LaFosse & Alexander's essential book of origami : the complete guide for everyone / by Michael G. LaFosse and Richard L. Alexander, Origamido, Inc.
Other titles: Essential book of origami | LaFosse and Alexander's essential book of origami
Description: Tokyo ; Rutland, Vermont : Tuttle Publishing, [2016]
Identifiers: LCCN 2016006735 | ISBN 9784805312681 (pbk.)
Subjects: LCSH: Origami.
Classification: LCC TT872.5 .L3325 2016 | DDC 736/.982--dc23 LC record available at https://lccn.loc.gov/2016006735

ISBN 978-4-8053-1268-1

Distributed by

North America, Latin America & Europe
Tuttle Publishing, 364 Innovation Drive, North Clarendon, VT 05759-9436 U.S.A.
Tel: (802) 773-8930 | Fax: (802) 773-6993
info@tuttlepublishing.com | www.tuttlepublishing.com

Japan
Tuttle Publishing, Yaekari Building, 3rd Floor, 5-4-12 Osaki, Shinagawa-ku, Tokyo 141 0032
Tel: (81) 3 5437-0171 | Fax: (81) 3 5437-0755
sales@tuttle.co.jp | www.tuttle.co.jp

Asia Pacific
Berkeley Books Pte. Ltd., 61 Tai Seng Avenue #02-12, Singapore 534167
Tel: (65) 6280-1330 | Fax: (65) 6280-6290
inquiries@periplus.com.sg | www.periplus.com

First edition
20 19 18 17 16   5 4 3 2 1   1606CM

Printed in China

ABOUT TUTTLE
"Books to Span the East and West"

Our core mission at Tuttle Publishing is to create books which bring people together one page at a time. Tuttle was founded in 1832 in the small New England town of Rutland, Vermont (USA). Our fundamental values remain as strong today as they were then—to publish best-in-class books informing the English-speaking world about the countries and peoples of Asia. The world has become a smaller place today and Asia's economic, cultural and political influence has expanded, yet the need for meaningful dialogue and information about this diverse region has never been greater. Since 1948, Tuttle has been a leader in publishing books on the cultures, arts, cuisines, languages and literatures of Asia. Our authors and photographers have won numerous awards and Tuttle has published thousands of books on subjects ranging from martial arts to paper crafts. We welcome you to explore the wealth of information available on Asia at **www.tuttlepublishing.com**.